M000096949

A Desirable Station

Soldier Life at Fort Mackinac, 1867-1895

A Desirable Station

Soldier Life at Fort Mackinac, 1867-1895

Phil Porter

Mackinac Island, Michigan

A Desirable Station
Soldier Life at Fort Mackinac, 1867-1895

by Phil Porter
Chief Curator
Mackinac State Historic Parks

©2003 Mackinac Island State Park Commission
All rights reserved

Art Director: Thomas Kachadurian

Mackinac State Historic Parks
P.O. Box 370
Mackinac Island, Michigan 49757

Library of Congress Cataloging-in-Publication Data

Porter, Phil, 1953-
  A Desirable Station : Soldier Life at Fort Mackinac, 1867-1895 / by
Phil Porter.
      p. cm.
Includes bibliographical references and index.
  ISBN 0-911872-82-5 -- ISBN 0-911872-81-7 (pbk.)
  1. Fort Mackinac (Mackinac Island, Mich.)--History--19th century. 2.
Soldiers--Michigan--Fort Mackinac (Mackinac Island)--History--19th
century. 3. United States. Army--Military life--History--19th century.
I. Title.
  F572.M16P668 2003
  355.7'09774'923--dc21

                                      2002154576

First Edition
First printing   3,000 copies, soft cover
                  2,000 copies, hard cover

Printed in the United States of America

To: David A. Armour

Historian, Mentor, Friend

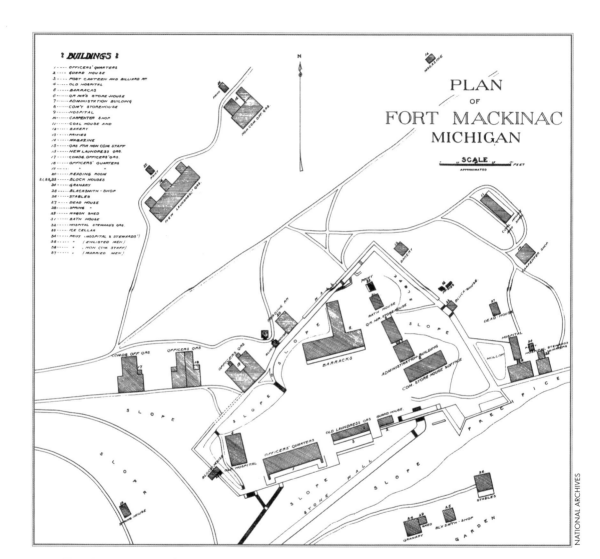

Fort Mackinac in 1890.

NATIONAL ARCHIVES

Table of Contents

Foreword

H ISTORIANS ARE KNOWN to spend hours, days or lives rooting through small details to develop understanding of the broad sweep of historical events, but museums have been uncertain to what extent the visiting public would do the same. For many years the staff of the Mackinac Island State Park Commission collected information about American soldiers who lived at Fort Mackinac, but until recently the detailed records were used only by researchers. In 1989 we opened the exhibition *Victorian Soldiers at Mackinac* and included data from muster roll and enlistment records for some of the soldiers. We were delighted to find our guests fascinated by the records, searching for family names or places of origin, and commenting to one another about the lives of the soldiers. The soldier records revealed a personal side of history that is not often found in other sources.

Under the direction of Chief Curator Phil Porter, staff and volunteer researchers assembled the full set of muster roll and enlistment records for Fort Mackinac that are the basis of this exploration of soldier life on Michigan's fabled island outpost. Analysis of the combined records tells us about the origins, health, character and behavior of the soldiers, and opens a window to greater understanding of late nineteenth century America. When combined with photographs and archaeological evidence, and examined with understanding of the fourteen original buildings that survive at the fort, the documents are an extraordinary depiction of everyday life at Mackinac.

A Desirable Station: Soldier Life at Fort Mackinac 1867-1895 continues the long tradition of Mackinac Island State Park Commission publications that use outstanding collections of buildings, documents, artifacts and images to explore the unique history and stories of Mackinac. Since 1895 the Commission has worked diligently to preserve the natural and cultural heritage of the Straits of Mackinac region, and to

Fort Mackinac ca. 1870.

share that heritage with others. Park Commission Chairman Dennis O. Cawthorne and all of the commissioners have our sincere appreciation for their strong commitment to the preservation and interpretation of Mackinac heritage.

Carl R. Nold
Director, Mackinac State Historic Parks
Mackinac Island State Park Commission

Introduction

My company goes to Fort Mackinac, Mich. on Mackinac Island, near the junction of Lakes Michigan and Huron. It is in the later. It is a fashionable summer resort but snowed in from the outside world during the winter when it is extremely cold. It is considered a desirable station; and we think we will like it.

Lieutenant Calvin D. Cowles
May 12, 1884

CAPTAIN JOHN MITCHELL and fifty-seven soldiers of Company B, Forty-third Regiment of Infantry took command of Fort Mackinac in August 1867. The Forty-third Infantry, a Veteran Reserve Corp regiment filled with wounded Civil War veterans, had limited capabilities – especially with the hard-drinking, trouble-ridden Mitchell in command. Fort Mackinac was the perfect place for this company. A strategically insignificant post for many years, the island fort had been abandoned since the beginning of the war except for a caretaker sergeant and occasional summer volunteer units.

Following the Civil War, Congress committed most of the army to enforcing the policies of Reconstruction in the south and supporting westward expansion beyond the Mississippi River. Fort Mackinac appeared to be doomed by obsolescence until summer vacationers rejuvenated the sagging post-fur-trade community of Mackinac Island which had been in decline since the 1830s. By the early 1870s tourism was the island's predominant industry and Fort Mackinac became a favorite stop for sightseers. More importantly, the island fort became the administrative headquarters of Mackinac National Park in 1875. The federal park breathed new life into the old fort as a second company of soldiers was added and a sense of purpose returned to the garrison.

The period between 1867 and 1895 was an exciting time for soldiers stationed at

The south sally port and south wall of Fort Mackinac ca. 1865.

Fort Mackinac. There was little fear of attack, drill and fatigue duties were light, modern conveniences abounded, and the burgeoning resort community offered plenty of exciting diversions for soldiers who received liberal amounts of free time. Many soldiers ordered to Fort Mackinac had the same reaction as Lieutenant Calvin D. Cowles who was pleasantly surprised and anxious to move to this "desirable station." After a grueling two thousand-mile journey from Fort Craig, New Mexico with his wife and five children, Cowles was not disappointed. Writing to his father in July 1884, he commented "I like this place first rate. My quarters are good and duties agreeable. I think I can stand four years of it very well."[1]

Chapter I

Setting the Stage: Fort Mackinac, 1781-1865

BRITISH SOLDIERS under the command of Lieutenant Governor Patrick Sinclair constructed Fort Mackinac during the American Revolution. Concerned about a possible attack from American soldiers and uncertain about the loyalty of neighboring Indians, Sinclair abandoned Fort Michilimackinac (Mackinaw City) and built a new fort on Mackinac Island's well-protected southern bluff in 1781. In searching for a more defensible location, Sinclair was committed to staying in the strategic Straits of Mackinac where he could protect upper Great Lakes shipping lanes, police the fur trade and maintain tribal alliances.

Fort Mackinac continued to meet these strategic objectives after it became a United States post following the American victory in the Revolution. In 1796 army commander General Anthony Wayne described Fort Mackinac as a post of "the first consequence" because of its importance to the military, commercial and diplomatic success of the Northwest Territory. With potentially hostile populations in Canada to the north and in Indian territory to the west, Fort Mackinac served as a crucial link in a chain of Great Lakes posts protecting the border. By 1803 Fort Mackinac was the nation's sixth largest post with more than 120 soldiers.

Great Britain continued to recognize the strategic value of the Straits of Mackinac and made the capture of Fort Mackinac a primary objective during the War of 1812. The fort's vulnerability was exposed early in the war when Captain Charles Roberts led a force of British soldiers and Indian warriors to the high ground behind the post on July 17, 1812. Fort Mackinac's unsuspecting American commander, Lieutenant Porter Hanks, quickly surrendered to Robert's well-positioned, superior force. Occupying British soldiers soon constructed Fort George on the island's high ground to protect

Sept. 1817. — *Michillimackinac from Round Island.* — *F.S. Bolton*

Fort Mackinac and Fort Holmes are prominently featured in this 1817 painting of Mackinac Island, by F.S. Bolton.

Fort Mackinac's weak side and guard against an American counter attack. The smaller post was later renamed Fort Holmes to honor Major Andrew Hunter Holmes who was killed during the disastrous American attempt to recapture the island in 1814.

American soldiers returned to Fort Mackinac in 1815 and resumed their pre-war tasks of policing the border, enforcing United States trade policies and nurturing alliances with area Indians. The island's commercial significance soared when John Jacob Astor established his American Fur Company's northern department headquarters on the island. Located in the center of the Great Lakes water highway system which connected the fur-bearing regions of the upper Midwest with East Coast and European markets, Mackinac became Astor's largest and most important depot. Through his political connections Astor lobbied to have Fort Mackinac soldiers protect his commercial interests. In 1816 Deputy Secretary of War George Graham expressed the government's desire to support the company's work at Mackinac when he ordered post commander Lieutenant Colonel John McNeil to "give to these gentlemen every possible facility and aid in the prosecution of their business that may be compatible with your public duties." On the one hand this meant protecting Astor's turf by keeping Canadian fur traders from doing business in United States territory. On the other hand, soldiers helped the United States Indian Agent regulate the fur trade – including the activities of Astor's free-wheeling American Fur Company. In either case, as long as the fur trade prospered, the government maintained a strong garrison at Fort Mackinac.

United States, Fort & village of Michilimackinac {Chippeway Indians encamped to State of Michigan...

Native American wigwams line the shore in this 1842 painting of Mackinac Island.

The decline of the fur trade in the 1830s was one of many factors that convinced the United States army to reconsider the importance of manning Fort Mackinac. Astor sold the American Fur Company in 1834 and the new owners diversified the firm and began commercial fishing operations on Lake Superior. Company president Ramsey Crooks shifted headquarters to LaPointe, Wisconsin and Mackinac Island ceased to be the company's main distribution center for the upper Great Lakes. As the nation expanded westward Fort Mackinac decreased in strategic value and contributed little to national defense. Fort Brady, constructed at Sault Ste. Marie in 1822, assumed responsibility for guarding the Canadian border and Fort Mackinac was reduced to the role of "strategic troop reserve" – a place to store soldiers until they were needed elsewhere. To this end the army sent Fort Mackinac soldiers to fight in the Second Seminole War (1837-1840), the Mexican War (1848), the Santee Indian uprising (1857-1858) and in support of the Union during the Civil War (1861-1865). When the post was reoccupied in between these conflicts the army usually assigned only one company of soldiers, half the size of the fur-trade-era garrison.

Chapter II

The U.S. Army and Fort Mackinac, 1867 – 1895

A T THE END OF THE CIVIL WAR the army struggled with the challenge of meeting new responsibilities while caring for many old facilities like Fort Mackinac. Soldiers from the 4th Independent Veteran Reserve Corp occupied the fort during the summer of 1866 before Congress authorized a substantial increase to the size of the regular army. Most of these soldiers were committed to post-Civil War policing of the south and supporting the nation's relentless expansion west through Indian lands. It was an indication of the army's lack of interest in Fort Mackinac that they assigned Captain Mitchell's company of wounded Civil War veterans of the Forty-third Infantry as the fort's first, full time, post-bellum garrison. The military was not quite ready to scrap the old fort, but there was little passion for keeping it. Nevertheless, the fort remained occupied and even survived the army's 1869 reduction when several regiments, including Veteran Reserves, were eliminated.

In June 1869 Captain Leslie Smith's First Infantry company took command of Fort Mackinac. Smith's soldiers manned a post that had survived nearly forty years of troop reduction, abandonment and neglect as it decreased in strategic value. Stone revetment walls, badly decayed and threatening to collapse at any moment, established the perimeter of the old fort. Three stone and heavy timber blockhouses on the north, east and west walls, originally constructed to protect the garrison, now served as storehouses and temporary barracks. Logs from the palisade walls that once connected the blockhouses and enclosed the fort had been taken down and used to cover the crumbling stone walls. The fort's artillery, consisting of two 6-pounder and two 12-pounder field guns and one 12-pounder howitzer, were mounted on the upper and lower gun platforms. An imposing 10" siege mortar was on the parade ground just inside the south sally port.

Fort Mackinac ca. 1865. The crumbling stone walls reflect years of disuse and neglect during the Civil War.

Most of the fort buildings surrounded the interior parade ground where the soldiers assembled, drilled and conducted weekly dress parade. Captain Smith and another senior officer lived in the ancient but solid stone quarters on the front bluff overlooking the harbor. Lieutenants occupied the hill quarters which was perched above the parade ground near the main flag staff. Enlisted men lived on the first floor of the soldiers barracks which had a washroom, dining room and kitchen in the back wing. Smith discovered that the once-elegant chapel on the second floor of the barracks had been vandalized by Captain Mitchell's soldiers who destroyed the altar and demolished the pews. Laundresses and their husbands, usually non-commissioned officers, lived in the wood quarters.

The other buildings around the parade ground included the guardhouse, headquarters, quartermaster's storehouse and old hospital now used by the quartermaster as a storage building. The stone powder magazine, in the southeast corner of the fort was so damp that gunpowder stored inside quickly spoiled. As a result, Captain Smith used the east blockhouse as a temporary magazine and ordnance storage building.

Some of the fort's newer buildings were constructed outside the fort walls. The hospital, bakery, privy and carpenter shop were just beyond the east wall while the ice house and water well were to the north. The stable and granary were to the south below the fort next to the five-acre military garden where soldiers grew fresh vegetables to supplement their bland military ration. Technologically, the fort had advanced little since it was built during the Revolution. The men used pit toilets, heated their quarters with wood and slept on wooden bunk beds with straw-filled mattresses. They hauled water from the lake in horse-drawn carts and communicated with the outside world through weekly mail service during the navigation season (May through November) and bi-weekly service during the winter.[2]

Critics called for the fort to be closed and Smith's men carried out their duties with little sense of purpose. They patrolled the walls (although there was little fear of attack), drilled on the parade ground (sharpening military skills unneeded at Mackinac) and repaired the fort's deteriorating structures (for an uncertain future). Though contributing little to national defense, Fort Mackinac survived this period of obsolescence and was poised to take a new role in the island's burgeoning post-war tourist economy.

Tourism became the business of Mackinac Island following the Civil War. Americans sought romantic and peaceful summer places to escape congested cities and forget the horror of war. With its historic charm, natural beauty and healthy environment, Mackinac Island was a perfect vacation spot. By the early 1870s an expanding railroad system and improved passenger boats brought great crowds to Mackinac. New hotels, curio shops and restaurants catering to the traveling masses sprang up along Main Street and filled the narrow back lanes. Some feared that commercial development would soon destroy Mackinac Island's unique charm and rustic beauty.

In 1873 the United States Senate directed the War Department to study the possibility of creating a national park on Mackinac Island. The bill was introduced by Michigan Senator Thomas W. Ferry just one year after Congress created Yellowstone National Park, the first national park in the country. Secretary of War William Belknap and his staff carefully studied the issue and responded favorably to Ferry's suggestion. After lengthy debate, the bill creating Mackinac National Park was passed by both houses of Congress and signed into law by President Ulysses S. Grant on March 3, 1875.

The presence of Fort Mackinac was crucial to success of the bill. While the project's detractors argued that the country could ill afford the expense of caring for a summer park on Mackinac Island, supporters reasoned that the fort's soldiers could supply much of the needed labor. The park was placed under the jurisdiction of the War Department and Secretary Belknap, in turn, appointed fort commander Major Alfred L. Hough as Park Superintendent. The seemingly antiquated and useless fort had a new lease on life.

Major Hough and his successors held the dual responsibilities of commanding the fort and managing the country's second national park. As superintendent, Hough enforced park rules and regulations, constructed new roads and trails, leased land for cottage construction, managed park funds and maintained a steady stream of correspondence with the War Department. It soon became clear that a single company of soldiers was inadequate to both garrison the fort and run the park. Further, the prestige

Quartermaster Sergeant John Fletcher, his wife Sarah and their children in front of the sergeant's quarters behind Fort Mackinac, 1891.

of national park status gave Fort Mackinac a "special character and importance" and the army wanted to be sure that the post presented an impressive, efficient and quality appearance to park visitors.[3]

In May 1876 the army sent a second company of soldiers to Fort Mackinac and began to enlarge and improve the fort. This phase of new construction, begun in 1876 and continued for the next fifteen years, dramatically improved the appearance of the fort and living conditions of its soldiers. Two elegant new officers' quarters were constructed on the bluff just west of the fort in 1876. A single family dwelling became the commandant's home and the duplex next door housed the post surgeon and a company commander. The following year the sergeants' quarters duplex was constructed on the rear parade ground outside the fort. Occupied primarily by departmental staff non-commissioned officers, the building was expanded to include a third apartment in 1885 when the first quartermaster sergeant was assigned to the fort. The new laundress' quarters, constructed in 1877 next to the sergeants' quarters, provided housing for married enlisted men and their families. Ten years later the steward's quarters was built next to the post hospital to accommodate Hospital Corps staff.[4]

At the same time that the army constructed new quarters they also made significant improvements to older residences. The officers' hill quarters was expanded and remodeled in 1874-75. A few years later the soldiers' barracks was enlarged and the second floor chapel converted into a squad room to accommodate the second company of soldiers. Barracks remodeling continued into the 1880s when the army replaced rotting plaster with beaded Norway pine boards, improved air flow and ventilation and rebuilt the imposing, columned front porch.[5]

Along with new and improved housing, the army built several support structures at Fort Mackinac during this period. A brick powder magazine constructed north of the fort enabled soldiers to move their gunpowder from the east blockhouse, which was dangerously close to several buildings including the hospital. The old stone magazine was demolished and replaced by a spacious commissary for food storage in 1878. The following year a schoolhouse was constructed to provide educational opportunities for soldiers and their children. Several buildings, including a coal shed, scale house and morgue were constructed in the open ground east of the fort while a new blacksmith shop was built near the garden in front of the fort.

The army undertook projects designed to improve soldiers' morale and provide recreational opportunities. These projects were part of a broader attempt to improve army life for enlisted men beginning in the 1880s. Known as the Army Reform Movement, these measures instituted better training procedures, improved uniforms and living conditions and provided recreational opportunities.[6] The War Department officially approved the construction and use of canteens for the entertainment, recreation and amusement of enlisted men at military posts in 1889. Officers at Fort Mackinac quickly took advantage of the new policy and remodeled the wood quarters into the post canteen at a cost of $82.53. Opened on November 7, 1889, the canteen provided the men with two billiard rooms and a bar and lunch counter. The rooms were furnished with books, magazines and board games including backgammon, checkers, dominoes and chess. The walls were decorated with large, framed pictures including seven large Civil War battle scenes donated by West Bluff summer cottager Henry Leman. In the lunch room soldiers enjoyed ham and cheese sandwiches with imported Swiss cheese and French mustard, light wines and beer, including Schlitz of Milwaukee which was sold for "five-cents per glass – large size." Beer was the main source of profit while coffee was discontinued after three weeks for lack of interest. The canteen was immensely popular with the soldiers and enthusiastically supported by the officers who noticed an immediate improvement in morale and

behavior.[7] The fort administration also supported recreational activities by allowing soldiers to use the company boats in their free time and encouraging sporting activities, especially baseball.

While new construction improved fort facilities and soldier morale, technological innovations enhanced their quality of life. Living conditions in the soldiers' barracks squad rooms improved in the early 1870s when old wood-burning heaters and double-deck wooden bunks were replaced by coal stoves and single, iron-framed beds. The men continued to sleep on straw mattresses and wooden slats until 1885 when the army supplied them with wire spring bunk bottoms and five-inch thick, cotton-stuffed mattresses. Post Surgeon Dr. John Bailey was so impressed with the new bedding that he remarked, "Such accommodations are very much better than those furnished by ordinary hotels and may be

Dr. John R. Bailey served as Acting Assistant Surgeon at Fort Mackinac nine times between 1871 and 1895.

Cattle grazing in the government pasture with Fort Mackinac in the background, ca. 1892. Trinity Episcopal Church is to the right and the fort pump house is on the far left.

said to be truly luxurious. They are conducive to sweet repose, comfort, cleanliness, contentment and health."[8]

Water supply to the fort improved dramatically in 1881 when a new water pumping and storage system was installed. Using a coal-powered hot air engine, fresh water was pumped from a spring below the fort to a 65-barrel reservoir constructed on the second floor of the North Blockhouse. In 1883 soldiers ran the pump two hours every morning, except for Sundays, to fill the water tank. From here water flowed through one-inch pipes to several buildings beginning with the mess rooms in the soldiers' barracks.[9] Eventually several buildings were connected to the water system including the post bathhouse constructed "in a hygiene fever" during the fall of 1885. Dr. Bailey described the new building as "the most useful at the post." It featured six cast iron bath tubs and hot and cold running water. The soldiers, Bailey boasted, "bathe once a week, or more, and their habits are generally cleanly."[10] Four years later plumbing contractors Sproul and McGurrin of Grand Rapids installed the fort's first water closets and flush toilets. Post Commander Captain Greenleaf A. Goodale gave his soldiers, most of whom were unfamiliar with this modern addition, detailed instructions to use only "soft paper" and avoid throwing matches, toothpicks and cigar stumps in the privy bowls. Violators, he warned, would be court martialed and made to use the old privies.[11]

The addition of telegraphy improved communications at Fort Mackinac beginning in July 1883. An underwater wire from St. Ignace ran to a single station in the island village operated by Miss Maggie Donnelly. A line was run from her office to Fort Mackinac so that officers could take advantage of this technology for communicating with the outside world. As a result, written correspondence from division headquarters in New York City that required seven to twenty-seven days of travel time by mail in the 1870s was replaced by instantaneous telegraphic service. Although most correspondence continued via mail, telegraphic communication proved very helpful in many situations. Such was the case when Private James Brown deserted on board the steam boat *Messenger* on June 6, 1886. Captain Greenleaf Goodale immediately telegraphed the news to the Cheboygan, Michigan city marshal. Because of this timely communication, civil authorities met the boat, arrested Brown and held him until Sergeant George Robinson escorted him back to Fort Mackinac two days later. Brown was convicted by a garrison court martial and sentenced to forfeit five dollars of his pay.[12]

Captain Greenleaf A. Goodale. Goodale served as Fort Mackinac post commandant from 1886 to 1890.

While soldiers kept busy with numerous construction projects in and around the fort, they were unable to work on most national park projects. At issue was the War Department's refusal to approve extra duty pay for soldiers working in the park. As a result, commandants did little to improve the park until the mid-1880s when cottage lease payments and the sale of government land on nearby Bois Blanc Island finally put money into the park coffers. Even then, the commandant was unable to use this money to pay his own men and was forced to hire contractors to construct roads, add fences, build stairways and make other park improvements.

Consequently, when not working on fort projects the soldier's day was filled with repetitive, but easy, military tasks. Guard, fatigue and police duty kept most men busy while others worked as bakers, tailors, nurses and cooks. Soldiers drilled regularly to hone their skills in bayonet practice, the manual of arms, marching and battle formations. Rifle skills were sharpened on the island's two target ranges.

Soldiers and the old fort became one of the island's premier tourist attractions. Curious visitors were allowed to tour the fort where they inspected the historic buildings, witnessed the guard mounting, walked along the Revolutionary-era ramparts and reveled in the atmosphere of nostalgia and patriotism. Evening dress parade was one of the most popular activities often drawing large crowds.[13] Concerned about the interaction of his soldiers and the day tourists, Major Hough issued strict orders in 1878 that visitors were to be treated politely and given free access to the grounds. On the other hand, Hough instructed his guards to eject "rowdys or loafers" and he forbade visitors from entering the guard house or talking to prisoners.[14]

By the late 1880s Mackinac Island became the most fashionable resort in the upper Great Lakes. Construction of the Grand Hotel, addition of palatial cottages and a multitude of other improvements propelled Mackinac and its historic fort to new prominence. Soldiers generally enjoyed their time at Fort Mackinac during this period, especially those who had served in lonely Western outposts where the threat of attack, lack of amenities and brutal weather conditions diminished their excitement for military service. The move to Mackinac was particularly appealing to their families who enjoyed the island's numerous material, social and educational advantages. Fanny Corbusier, wife of Post Surgeon Dr. William Corbusier, was thrilled to find that her rooms were heated with coal-burning stoves and lit with kerosene lamps. Community activities included dances at the John Jacob Astor House, magic lantern exhibitions at Truscott's Hall and a wide variety of recreational opportunities from sledding in the winter to beach picnics on nearby Round Island in the summer. Fanny sent her children to the post school and worshipped at Trinity Episcopal Church where her husband served on the vestry.[15]

Elegant West Bluff cottages with Grand Hotel in the distance, ca. 1905.

Aerial view of Fort Mackinac with island harbor in the background.

As soldiers increasingly enjoyed life at Fort Mackinac, army administrators grew ever more skeptical of its military worth. They had the same opinion of Fort Mackinac as tourists; it was a charming curiosity, and little more. In an effort to save money and consolidate troops, the army abandoned dozens of small, less-strategic forts beginning in the late 1880s. By 1892 the army manned only 96 forts, down from a post-Civil War high of 255 forts in 1869.[16] Fort Mackinac dodged the fatal bullet for several years because it provided administrative support for the national park. But at a cost of forty to fifty thousand dollars a year, the old fort eventually became a sitting target for sharp-eyed army budget trimmers. The first cut came in November 1892 when Company D, Nineteenth Infantry was sent to Fort Brady. Two years later Secretary of War Daniel Lamont withdrew most of the remaining troops. Lieutenant Woodbridge Geary and a squad of eleven men stayed behind until the government decided on the final disposition of the fort and national park. Lamont's proposal to sell park lands shocked local citizens who scurried to preserve their island and found a willing advocate in Senator James McMillan. McMillan led the effort to save the park by transferring it to the State of Michigan. Congress approved the transfer in March 1895. Six months later Lieutenant Geary and his small squad of soldiers marched out of Fort Mackinac for the last time.

Chapter III

Soldiers of Fort Mackinac, 1867 - 1895

Enlisted Men - Soldier Profile

MORE THAN ONE THOUSAND SOLDIERS, including enlisted men, officers and departmental staff, served at Fort Mackinac between 1867 and 1895.[17] These soldiers served in infantry regiments which were assigned to Great Lakes forts, usually for five year terms.[18] An average of forty to fifty soldiers manned the post during the first nine years. This number doubled after a second company of soldiers was added in the Mackinac National Park years. From a peak of about 115 soldiers in the late 1880s the fort's population declined until it was closed, especially after the second company was removed in 1892. Throughout this period the fort's population also included a number of non-military residents, primarily soldiers' families and civilian employees.

The soldiers who served at Fort Mackinac during these years were part of an all-volunteer army with an average strength of about 25,000 men. Soldiers enlisted in the army for different reasons. Some looked for excitement while others sought refuge. Whether they were Indiana farm boys or Irish immigrants, frightened businessmen running from a sour deal or wide-eyed warriors aching for adventure, most enlistees joined the army because it provided steady work and sure pay. Once in the army soldiers could count on three square meals a day, a roof over their heads and a steady, though modest, monthly salary.

The army used diverse recruiting practices to attract prospective soldiers. Permanent recruiting stations were established in large cities, especially in the Middle Atlantic, Northeast and Midwest. These recruiting stations were manned by a rotation of officers from posts around the country including Fort Mackinac. Although a great many

Fort Mackinac soldiers at dress parade in front of the soldiers' barracks, ca. 1890.

soldiers joined the army at these recruiting stations, officers bemoaned the "class of men" that they produced. Colonel Richard Dodge, a veteran infantry officer with nearly forty years experience, argued that big city recruits were "very frequently of the 'rough and tough' element, lazy, intemperate, vicious and reckless."[19]

Soldiers enlisted at permanent recruiting stations were usually sent to recruit depots to await assignment to specific regiments. Newport Barracks, Kentucky, David's Island, New York and Columbus Barracks, Ohio served as infantry depots that sent soldiers to Fort Mackinac. Soldiers spent anywhere from a few days to several months at depots before they were shipped out. Of the twenty-two recruits sent from David's Island to Fort Mackinac in August 1883 all but two joined the army within the prior three months.[20] Although originally intended as way stations for recruits, the depots were used as training centers beginning in the 1880s. Here, the inexperienced soldier received his first uniform, tasted his first army ration, learned basic drills and experienced the rough edge of military discipline and order. Life in the depots was often an unpleasant experience and recruits were usually eager to move on to permanent assignments.[21]

The army also enlisted soldiers through direct recruiting by regiments. Regimental recruiting often focused on smaller towns where, Colonel Dodge argued, "the character of each applicant for enlistment can be thoroughly ascertained."[22] A regimental recruiting detail in Jackson, Michigan sent fourteen raw recruits to Fort Mackinac in March 1892. Most of these men came from small towns in Michigan and the surrounding states.[23]

Soldiers also were recruited at Fort Mackinac, especially after the mid-1880s when commandants regularly assigned this duty to a junior officer. In 1883 Lieutenant Walter Duggan enlisted eight recruits to fill vacancies in the Tenth Infantry companies at Fort Mackinac. This diverse group included two Canadians, one Russian, one Swede and one Norwegian as well as a native of New York state and Cleveland-born brothers George and Lewis Goodrich. Before enlisting the men Duggan explained their pay and clothing allowances, warned them of the punishment for desertion and marched them to the post hospital where Dr. Corbusier gave them a complete physical examination.[24]

Walter Duggan.

Two years later Lieutenant Edward Pratt became the fort's recruiting officer for the Twenty-third Infantry. During his four year stint Pratt reenlisted many soldiers already serving at the fort but signed up only two new recruits.[25] His successors with the Nineteenth Infantry were a little more successful as they enrolled six volunteers in the early 1890s.[26] While these local efforts did not produce the number of enlistees garnered through general and regimental recruitment, they did help supplement the ranks. Soldiers enlisted through regimental and post efforts were generally able to avoid the recruit depots and received their training once they arrived on the island.

The army recorded important information about every soldier at the time he joined. The "Register of Enlistments" provides valuable information that puts a human face on the Fort Mackinac community. Included in the register is the birth country of each soldier. Fort Mackinac enlisted men between 1867 and 1895 hailed from twenty-two different countries and thirty-three different states and the District of Columbia. The nineteenth-century army always had a sizeable number of immigrants and in the first ten years after the Civil War foreign-born recruits accounted for about 50 percent of the enlisted population. The percentage steadily declined to less than 18 percent in 1895.[27] This was the pattern at Fort Mackinac where the immigrant population totaled 51 percent between 1867 and 1879 and dwindled to 32 percent during the last five years. Reflecting general immigration patterns, the largest number of foreign-born soldiers in the army came from Ireland and Germany. Again, the pattern held true at Fort Mackinac where Irishmen (42 percent) and Germans (26 percent) dominated the foreign-born population. Truly a cosmopolitan community during this period, Fort Mackinac soldiers also came from Canada, England, Scotland, Wales, Switzerland, Italy, France, Holland, Denmark, Norway, Sweden, Poland, Prussia, Austria, Bohemia, Russia, Greece, Turkey and Australia.[28]

United States-born soldiers came primarily from northern states from the East Coast to the Mississippi River, clearly a result of the location of permanent recruiting stations. New York and Pennsylvania supplied the most soldiers but Midwestern states, particularly Ohio and Michigan, sent an increasing number of soldiers to the fort in later years. Soldiers came to the fort from every state east of the Mississippi River (except Mississippi) as well as Minnesota, Iowa, Missouri, Arkansas, Nebraska, Kansas and Texas.[29]

The diverse enlisted population presented numerous challenges to post commanders. Besides dealing with language and cultural differences, fort officers also had to contend with occasional rifts between men from different nations. Although there was undoubtedly much good natured teasing and mild name calling in the relaxed atmosphere of the soldiers' barracks, bigoted soldiers sometimes became abusive. Michigan-born Private Hugh Stevenson faced a summary court martial in August 1892 for being drunk and disorderly in his company quarters and for calling German-born Private Alfred Schnell a "damn dutch son of a bitch." Sergeant Frederick Shulte encountered a similar drunken outburst after taking a flask of whiskey from Canadian native Private Henry Pedigrew. Pedigrew found himself in front of a military court for threatening retaliation and calling Shulte a "dutch son of a bitch and a dutch Bastard." That same year Irish-born privates Martin Curley and Martin Boyle faced charges when they insulted their American-born non-commissioned officers. Curley was court martialed for, among other charges, calling Indiana native Sergeant James Martin a "damned Hoosier" and Boyle was arrested for using equally abusive language while proudly proclaiming his Irish ancestry.[30]

These examples are exceptions rather than the rule. Fort officers kept national rivalries to a minimum by maintaining a low tolerance for abuse and high level of

1880's soldiers on the Fort Mackinac parade ground. Note the young child with the first sergeant on the left.

company discipline. By way of example to their troops, Fort Mackinac officers showed little prejudice when promoting men to non-commissioned ranks. In fact, the percentage of foreign-born non-commissioned officers was generally equal to or higher than the percentage of foreign-born in the total enlisted population. Further, officers showed no preference to any particular nationality as men from fifteen different foreign countries served as non-commissioned officers during this period.

One issue that Fort Mackinac officers did not have to face was racial prejudice. Despite the remarkable diversity of the enlisted population, no black soldiers ever served at Fort Mackinac. Blacks in the United States army during this period served in segregated regiments: the Twenty-fourth and Twenty-fifth Infantry and Ninth and Tenth Cavalry, all with white officers.

The "Register of Enlistments" also recorded the age of every enlisting soldier. The soldiers who served at Fort Mackinac during this period were between sixteen and eighty-four years old. Most men were in their twenties with seasoned veterans and non-commissioned officers usually being a little older. The oldest group was Captain Mitchell's Reserve Corp company, all wounded Civil War veterans who averaged about twenty-eight years. The men in Captain Leslie Smith's company who replaced them in 1869 were, on average, four years younger.[31]

Fort Mackinac's youngest soldiers were musicians. Theodore Reiths, John Monroe and John Reynolds were all younger than eighteen when they came to Mackinac. Reiths began his military career as a twelve-year old Civil War musician and he arrived

at Fort Mackinac as a seasoned seventeen-year old bugler in 1869. Monroe's parents died when he was thirteen years old and he was forced to work as a farm laborer until he joined the army three years later as a bugler. While he was still only sixteen years old Monroe was convicted by a general court martial of stealing another soldier's paycheck. Monroe was dishonorably discharged from the service and sentenced to spend six months in the Fort Mackinac guardhouse. He escaped twice from confinement and was finally apprehended in Columbus, Ohio and sentenced to five years at Fort Leavenworth, Kansas military prison.[32]

On the other end of the age scale were Fort Mackinac's middle-aged veterans. All of these men, including Patrick McCormick, were multi-term career soldiers. McCormick, a five-foot, four-inch tall, Irish-born private, was forty-seven years old when he came to Fort Mackinac in 1890. He was in his sixth enlistment having joined the army twenty-six years earlier as a volunteer with the 70th Ohio Infantry during the Civil War. McCormick reenlisted in 1893 and concluded his army career two years later while he was still at Fort Mackinac.[33]

Because he had over thirty years of service, McCormick was able to officially retire and collect three-quarters of his pay and allowances. The army retirement benefit was approved by Congress only ten years earlier. Prior to 1885 enlisted men received no retirement benefits except a bed in the Soldiers' Home in Washington, D.C. if they were disabled in the line of duty or had served at least twenty years in the regular army.[34] Occasionally the army promoted long-serving and faithful soldiers to the rank of second lieutenant, thereby enabling them to receive the retirement due commissioned officers. Captain Leslie Smith petitioned the adjutant general to grant such a promotion to Ordnance Sergeant William Marshall, Fort Mackinac's oldest and longest-serving soldier.

Marshall joined the army in 1823 and came to Fort Mackinac twenty-five years later as post ordnance sergeant. The "Old Sergeant," as he was known to all in his later years, was the sole caretaker of Fort Mackinac when it was abandoned during the Civil War. In 1871 Captain Smith, citing Marshall's "singularly long and faithful term of service," requested a promotion for the seventy-one year old sergeant so that his remaining years might be "passed in ease and comfort which he so well deserves." The army denied Smith's request and Marshall continued to serve at Fort Mackinac until his death in 1884, one year before the army retirement program was enacted.[35]

The "Register of Enlistments" also recorded the height, eye color, hair color and complexion of every soldier. These physical descriptions were used to help identify soldiers killed in action or, much more often, those who deserted. From this data we learn that the average Fort Mackinac soldier between 1867 and 1895 stood a little over five-feet, seven-inches tall. The shortest soldiers, at slightly more than five-feet, six- inches tall, were the men of Company F, First Infantry (1869-1874). Twenty years later the fort's tallest soldiers, Company D, Nineteenth Infantry, marched into Fort Mackinac standing nearly five-feet, eight-inches tall.[36]

Enlisted Men – Ranks, Responsibilities and Remuneration

Enlisted men, including privates, musicians, corporals and sergeants, comprised the majority population of Fort Mackinac. Typical is the ratio of Company C, Twenty-second Infantry, which counted twenty privates, two musicians, four corporals, five sergeants, two lieutenants and one captain on the January 1877 post return.[37] Privates were the backbone of the army. Whether it was fighting in the field, marching sentry beats, policing the grounds or working on fatigue duty, privates did most of the work. Fort Mackinac privates, mostly in their early to mid-twenties, came to the army

The Fort Mackinac Military Band poses for a group shot in the island village, ca. 1877.

with a wide variety of employment backgrounds. There were clerks and shoemakers, butchers and bakers, blacksmiths and horse trainers, carpenters and harness makers, teamsters and cowboys, stone cutters and printers, miners and barbers. Most were unskilled laborers and farmers. [38]

Fort Mackinac musicians were drummers, buglers and fifers. Most of the daily duty calls were played on drum and bugle, instruments that were clearly heard throughout the garrison. Fifers, when available, added a nice melodic accompaniment to marches and ceremonial occasions and also played duty calls when needed. A few recruits were experienced musicians including Edward Lang, Charles Kegelmeyer, William Romans and the Bohemian-born brasstuner Albert Kwasnicka. Most musicians, however, came with some skill but little experience. Cigarmaker Jacob Herzog, gardener George Turner and laborers James Merrill and Max Minosky all became musicians after they joined the army – some pressed into service with short notice. When Lieutenant Dwight Kelton realized that he was losing both of his musicians in the spring of 1883 he quickly assigned Harry Laundenslager to daily duty "learning music." Less than three months later Laundenslager became the company's sole musician. [39]

Officers promoted dependable, sober and efficient privates to the important ranks of corporal and sergeant. These non-commissioned officers played a key role in the daily administration and supervision of the company. Officers gave the orders and "noncoms," who served entirely at the pleasure of the company commander, made sure that they were carried out. Noncoms oversaw guard duty, transported military convicts, supervised work crews, served as canteen stewards and worked as clerks in the company office and in the quartermaster and commissary departments.

The first sergeant held a role of particular importance as he was senior enlisted man in the company. Only twenty different men served as company first sergeants at Fort Mackinac during this period. Commanders filled this position with savvy veterans who had extensive military service and the toughness to keep twenty to thirty privates and noncoms in order. Captain Charles Webb described the ideal candidate for the job when he evaluated his long-serving First Sergeant George Cartright as "A man of excellent habits, a thorough soldier and a competent man."[40] Career soldiers, who could bring stability and longevity to this position, were particularly valuable. Thomas Ferris, a seasoned veteran with Civil War experience, served as first sergeant during his company's entire five-year stay at Fort Mackinac. Ferris continued to hold this rank for another five years after he left Mackinac until he died of consumption at Fort Davis, Texas in 1879.[41] Most first sergeants earned the genuine respect and gratitude of their commanders but a few proved unworthy and suffered humiliating falls from grace. Scottish immigrant John Romanis was first sergeant at Fort Mackinac for nearly three years before a series of misadventures doomed him. Court martialed for sending Private Curley to town for liquor and letting men fight in the orderly room, Romanis was reduced to the rank of private where he remained during the rest of his enlistment.[42]

All of the enlisted men lived in the soldiers' barracks. Approximately fifteen to twenty-five privates and musicians stayed in the large, central squad rooms on each

23rd Infantry soldiers relax in the first floor squad room of the Fort Mackinac soldiers' barracks, 1886.

23rd Infantry soldiers assembled in front of the soldiers' barracks, ca. 1886.

floor. Space was limited and personal possessions were few. Every soldier had a bunk, a foot locker and space on the wall behind his bed to store clothing and personal items. A few other sparse furnishings, including two heating stoves, gun racks, tables and chairs filled the remaining space in the cramped squad room. Noncoms enjoyed a little more privacy in smaller rooms on the ends of the building and first sergeants had the distinct privilege of a private room.

Departmental staff including ordnance, commissary and quartermaster sergeants and hospital stewards served at Fort Mackinac during this period. These men were not attached to the resident companies but were assigned to the fort from their departmental headquarters. Departmental staff had specific and limited garrison duties. Ordnance sergeants cared for the artillery, rifles, pistols, ammunition and related equipment. Besides the six pieces of artillery mounted on the fort walls, the ordnance sergeant's main responsibility was gunpowder storage and caring for the large supply of Springfield rifles. Nicknamed the "Trapdoor Springfield" because of its rising breech block, this rifle, with slight modifications, was used throughout the period. Commissary sergeants helped manage the fort's food supplies. Tons of food, from beef and bacon to coffee and fresh vegetables, was needed every year to feed Fort Mackinac's soldiers. Working out of a small office in the post commissary, the sergeant assisted an officer in receiving, storing and distributing the food. Likewise, the quartermaster sergeant assisted the officer in charge of military quarters, clothing, fuel, horses, wagons and other supplies and materials needed by the garrison. Hospital stewards made up prescriptions, administered medicines and generally supervised the sick under the direction of the post surgeon. Ordnance, commissary and quartermaster sergeants lived in non-commissioned officers' quarters behind the fort and stewards lived in the post hospital until an adjacent quarters was constructed for them in 1887.

Many staff non-commissioned officers had prior service as company sergeants. John Fletcher arrived at Fort Mackinac in 1885 with more than twenty years of military experience, fifteen as a sergeant. He was the fort's first quartermaster sergeant and held this position until he retired from the army eight years later. Most staff noncoms arrived at Fort Mackinac from other posts, but a few were promoted from within including sergeants Edward Raymond and George Sontheimer, the fort's first two commissary sergeants. Noncoms, even well-paid, esteemed first sergeants, eagerly jumped at the chance to transfer into departmental staff positions. For more than two years Boston native John Hooten enjoyed the respect of his commanders and faithfulness of his enlisted men as Company D Tenth Infantry first sergeant. He shared comfortable quarters with his wife Marie and even earned enough to employ a live-in servant.[43] He willingly traded his prestigious position at Fort Mackinac to join the Commissary Department on October 17, 1881 and was shipped out three days later to serve as commissary sergeant at Fort Livingston, Louisiana. First sergeants Alexander Kaufman and John Anness also left Fort Mackinac to take staff positions elsewhere. The primary inducements were less responsibility and more pay.

John Fletcher served as Fort Mackinac's first quartermaster sergeant from 1885 to 1893.

The starting pay for Fort Mackinac enlisted men during this period was between $13 and $34 per month. First year privates earned $13 per month, corporals $15, duty sergeants $17 and first sergeants $22. The quartermaster sergeant was paid $23 per month, hospital stewards between $20 and $30 and ordnance and commissary sergeants $34.[44] From this pay the government deducted 12 cents from each soldier to support the Soldiers Home. The post commandant also subtracted a sum from each soldier as set by a council of administration, usually between 50 cents and $1 per month, to pay the post laundresses.

Pay rates were higher during the Civil War when the scale began at $16 a month for privates. When Congress reduced the scale to pre-war levels in 1871 the rank and file expressed their opinions in a desertion rate which soared from 9.4 percent to 32.6

percent.[45] The reaction at Fort Mackinac was not quite so dramatic but during the summer of 1871 Captain Leslie Smith lost nine men to desertion, about sixteen percent of the enlisted population.

In response to rampant desertions, Congress enacted legislation in May 1872 to improve soldiers' compensation. Base pay rates were not raised, but the new law provided for annual increases of $1 per month beginning in the third year of a soldier's first enlistment. Soldiers also received a bonus for reenlistment. The private who began his army career at $13 a month now earned $16 a month by the end of his first enlistment and began his second enlistment at $18 per month. The pay for noncoms and departmental staff was raised accordingly and, along with private's pay, remained essentially unchanged until 1898.[46] Soldiers appreciated the pay raise but chaffed at the provision that all income above the base pay would be retained by the government until the soldier received an honorable discharge. Retained pay, the army reasoned, rewarded the faithful soldier and discouraged the would-be deserter. Soldiers at Fort Mackinac took a different view and Captain Smith lost an additional fourteen men to desertion in 1872. "This command is so much reduced by desertions," Smith complained on July first, "that there are absolutely not men enough to perform the guard duty of one post. I have only seven privates for guard duty this morning."[47] The flow of desertions was not stemmed until the financial Panic of 1873 when jobs were hard to find and army enlistments increased.

Soldiers on police duty near the East Blockhouse. The fort's 10-inch siege mortar is in the foreground.

Extra duty pay helped soldiers supplement their base salaries. This additional pay was extended to soldiers working on special projects or assignments that lasted at least ten days. Beginning in 1884 mechanics, artisans and school teachers earned fifty cents per day while on extra duty and clerks, teamsters, laborers and others earned thirty-five cents. Non-commissioned officers earned extra pay only when working as overseers in charge of work crews of at least twenty men.[48] Considering that a first-year private earned about forty-three cents a day, extra duty was a highly prized and sought-after assignment that could easily double a soldier's monthly pay. Those chosen for extra duty often had special skills before they joined the army: mechanic William Wilson ran the water pumping engine, brick layer Duncan Monroe worked as a mason, saddler Gottfried Hillengahs repaired harnesses, blacksmith Hiram Eddy worked as an artificer and carpenter Frank Holman fixed wagons.[49]

Most extra duty assignments were for short term construction or maintenance projects, but some assignments required a longer commitment which brought substantial extra income. Private Benedict Landau earned an additional fifty-cents a day for nearly a year while serving as post school teacher in 1887-1888. Three years later Private Patrick McCormick began working on extra duty as laborer in the subsistence department, a job that he kept for nearly three-and-a-half years.[50] Another benefit of extra duty was that it often exempted soldiers from unpopular routine duties including guard, drill, kitchen and police duty.

Not every skilled artisan who worked at Fort Mackinac received extra duty pay from the army. Soldiers on "daily duty" as tailors and shoemakers received payment directly from the soldiers for whom they worked. Others, including Nineteenth Infantry musician Abraham Owen, earned extra money as barbers. Although not on "daily duty" Owen supplemented his pay by shaving beards and cutting hair in his free time.[51]

Pay day, regardless of the level of compensation, was cause for celebration in the garrison. Soldiers queued up outside the post headquarters where the paymaster set up a temporary office. One by one they filed through the office, signed the payroll and received their payment. Paymasters were scheduled to visit Fort Mackinac every two months, but frozen lakes limited travel to the fort in the winter. Soldiers often went several months without pay. This was remedied in January 1886 when the Michigan Central Railroad began winter service to Mackinaw City and Major Albert S. Tower brought paychecks to a delighted group of Fort Mackinac soldiers.[52]

Infrequent and irregular pay days meant that soldiers depended on a liberal use of credit from fellow soldiers and island merchants. Soldiers often owed each other money from loans or gambling losses. Avaricious money lenders sometimes charged exorbitant rates to vulnerable soldiers leaving them deeply in debt. To protect his garrison from these usurious soldiers, Captain Goodale established a maximum lending rate of two percent among the enlisted men. Soldiers disobeying this order, he warned, would be subject to general court martial.[53] Several businesses, including James Gallagher's grocery, Arnold Transit Line and J. W. Davis general merchandise store all extended credit to Fort Mackinac soldiers. Every merchant on the island knew when the paymaster arrived and soldiers had to quickly settle their debts in order to continue to receive credit from these establishments.

After the post canteen was added in 1889, downtown merchants had to wait in line for their money. Upon application, most Fort Mackinac soldiers were extended a line of credit at the post canteen. On pay day soldiers were ordered to "immediately" proceed from the paymaster to the canteen reading room where accumulated debts had to be paid. Private Edward Bruckner, barred from the canteen for failure to pay a $2.90 tab, snuck back into the canteen bar room and bought a beer on a cool March night in 1891. When confronted by the canteen steward, Bruckner lied about his out-

standing debt and was arrested, confined and court martialed. Bruckner's antics cost him an additional two dollars in fines and five days in the Post Guardhouse.[54]

A soldier's compensation also included a clothing allowance. Each soldier received an undress or fatigue uniform consisting of a dark blue fatigue blouse, woolen trousers, a forage cap, a campaign hat and leather boots. The dress uniform used the same trousers with a long dark blue coat and a helmet. Infantry uniform styles changed throughout the period. The surplus Civil War uniforms that soldiers wore in the late 1860s and early 1870s were replaced with Prussian-influenced dress uniforms featuring spiked helmets in the 1880s and 1890s. The army issued additional clothing including socks, shirts, suspenders, overcoats and fur caps and gauntlets. Soldiers drew uniform supplies against their annual clothing allowance from the post quartermaster. In order to encourage soldiers to take care of their clothing, the unused portion of the allowance was paid in cash upon discharge from the army. In January 1885 Sergeant James Martin received a forage cap, one pair trousers and four pairs of stockings valued at $3.47 against a clothing balance of nearly $40. Martin continued to spend less than his allowance and when he left the

Indiana native Sergeant James Martin served at Fort Mackinac from 1884 to 1891.

army in March 1891 the frugal soldier received a pay out of $61.13 in clothing savings.[55] Conversely, those soldiers who overdrew their clothing account had to pay the difference.

Enlisted men were constantly evaluated by company officers. In the tight confines of a small garrison like Fort Mackinac a soldier's behavior, both good and bad, was easy to monitor. While officers made daily judgements about everything from the cleanliness of a soldier's rifle to his sobriety on guard duty, the final and most important evaluation came at the end of his enlistment. This assessment not only determined a soldier's eligibility for reenlistment, but also provided a reference for future employers. Beginning in the late 1870s company commanders were required to give a written evaluation of each soldier on the "Character" line on the discharge form. The work of most soldiers was usually summed up with a single word: "Excellent," "Good," "Fair," or "Worthless." The term "Without Character" was reserved for the most ineffective soldiers who were not to be reenlisted.

As officers became more comfortable with this system of evaluation, their appraisals became more colorful and descriptive. Private Joseph Holloway was an "Inebriate" and his company mate Charles Stewart was "A thief." Several soldiers received a qualified vote of confidence including Henry Burnes who was "A clean soldier, an honest man. . . with fair habits" and Charles Packard whose fourteen garrison courts martial are explained by his evaluation: "Good, except when drinking." The most glowing evaluations were reserved for long-serving non-commissioned officers including sergeant and post school teacher Frederick J. Grant who was "Excellent, A good French Scholar" and thirty-three-year old First Sergeant Thomas Hennessey who was "Excellent, an intelligent, soldierly and efficient first sergeant."[56] Soldiers could formally object to their character evaluation and request reconsideration. Private James Martin's objection did him little good when he was discharged in March 1891 as a reviewing board of officers confirmed the "fair" evaluation given him by Lieutenant Edmund Smith.[57]

Occasionally officers even went so far as to write reference letters for departing soldiers. When Quartermaster Sergeant John Fletcher left Fort Mackinac after thirty years of army service, he carried with him a letter from Lieutenant Joseph Frazier praising him as "always sober and absolutely reliable" and recommending his "clerical ability to any firm who might see fit to employ you."[58]

Commissioned Officers – The Officer Corps

Fort Mackinac's commissioned officers, including majors, captains and lieutenants, were part of the United States Army officer corps that averaged about 2,000 men during the period 1867 to 1895. These men served by virtue of a presidential commission received through civilian appointment, graduation from the United States Military Academy at West Point or promotion from the enlisted ranks. Officers from all three sources served at Fort Mackinac.

Civil War veterans dominated the officer corps for many years after the rebellion. Thirty-three of the fifty-four officers (61%) who served at Fort Mackinac during the period 1867-1895 were Civil War veterans. This group included regular army officers who remained in service after the war and volunteers who mustered out of their militia units at the end of the war and rejoined by appointment in the late 1860s. Their war experiences had a profound impact on their service at Fort Mackinac.

Many officers with Civil War experience understood the challenges and frustrations of the enlisted man's daily routine from personal experience. George Brady, Greenleaf Goodale, Walter Duggan, Edwin Gardner, Edwin Gaskill, Dwight Kelton and William Manning all began their military careers as privates. Goodale joined the Sixth Maine volunteers in 1861 as a twenty-two year old private and fought his way through Fredericksburg, Chancellorsville and Gettysburg. Goodale was promoted to sergeant in 1863 and, later that year, jumped at the opportunity to command African-American soldiers by accepting an officer's commission with the 77th United States Colored Troops.[59] After mustering out at the end of the war Goodale was commissioned as a first lieutenant in the regular army. Goodale, a deeply religious man, believed that he was spared injury during the war by the grace

Alfred Hough, shown here during his service with the 19th Infantry during the Civil War, served as post commandant at Fort Mackinac in the 1870s.

of God. Relying on that same deep faith, he chose his regiment by blindly pointing at a group of regimental crests in a Washington, D.C. army headquarters. His finger came to rest on the Twenty-third Infantry and he faithfully served that regiment for the next thirty-three years.[60]

Not every Fort Mackinac officer escaped the Civil War without injury. Many of these wounded veterans were constantly reminded of their great sacrifice, even years later while serving in the peaceful confines of Fort Mackinac. Edwin Gaskill was wounded while leading soldiers from the 36th United States Colored Troops during the New Market Heights operations in 1864. His injuries resulted in the amputation of his right arm. While at Fort Mackinac Gaskill met and married Elizabeth Disbrow. After retiring in 1870, the Gaskills returned to Mackinac Island where they raised a family and Edwin was elected president of the village. Gaskill suffered from his war wound almost continually and finally died on June 17, 1889 at age 45.[61] An impressive military procession escorted his body to the island's post cemetery two days later. William Manning was wounded twice during the war and carried a minie ball from Bull Run in his left hip for the rest of his life. John Mitchell was wounded before the war during an 1860 skirmish with Ute and Bannock Indians in Utah. He was wounded three more times during the war including an accidental, self-inflicted gunshot from his revolver. These painful wounds may have contributed to the chronic alcoholism that eventually took his life just six months after he left command of Fort Mackinac in 1869.[62]

Along with Civil War combat experience, several Fort Mackinac officers sharpened their military skills during the Indian Wars. William Manning received a brevet promotion for "gallant service in action against Indians at the Mazatzal Mountains on 13 December 1872." Edwin Coates and Edward B. Pratt both fought in the 1876-1877 Sioux Campaign. Calvin D. Cowles engaged the Northern Cheyenne in 1878 and the Uncompahgre Utes two years later. Charles Davis participated in Colonel Randal Mackenzie's 1878 incursion into Mexico in pursuit of hostile Indians and John McAdam Webster served in the Yellowstone Campaign with Colonel George A. Custer shortly before being sent to Fort Mackinac in 1874.[63] This combat duty gave Fort Mackinac officers valuable experience when training soldiers in skirmish exercises and target practice. That training was later used by soldiers who served on Western battlefields and in the Spanish American War and Philippine Insurrection.

In the 1880s United States Military Academy graduates began to replace the Civil War veterans who previously dominated the Fort Mackinac officer corps. While there were only two West Pointers at Fort Mackinac in the first decade after the Civil War, nine served at the island post

Henry Learned as a West Point cadet in 1890. Learned was assigned to Fort Mackinac soon after graduating from the academy.

during its last ten years. Slowly the fort's officer corps was shifting from those who had brief, but intense, combat experience during the war to those who had excellent academic training but little field experience. As a result, companies often had officers with widely varying backgrounds. Captain Jacob H. Smith, a sixty-year old Ohio-born veteran, wounded at the Battle of Shiloh in 1862 and promoted for gallant and meritorious service during the war, commanded Company D Nineteenth Infantry when they arrived on the island in 1890. His staff included three West Pointers none of whom had fought in the Civil War. The youngest, twenty-two year old Second Lieutenant Henry Grant Learned, was just out of the academy.[64]

Promotions during this period came very slowly, a particularly frustrating experience for the Civil War veterans who had enjoyed meteoric advancement while fighting in the Union army. During the war William Manning went from private to major in less than four years but when he joined the 14th Infantry in 1866 it took ten years before he was promoted. His next advancement came twenty-three years later just before he retired.[65] Performance was not the issue with Manning or most officers. The problem was that so many young men were commissioned at the same time that the lack of retirements meant that senior positions were not available. This frustration was shared by many Fort Mackinac officers of this period.

Post surgeons were an important part of the commissioned staff at Fort Mackinac during this period. Assigned to the post by the Army Medical Department, these physicians came from a variety of backgrounds. Five of the fort's twelve surgeons were medical officers during the Civil War where they received valuable, if harrowing, experience in field hospitals. Typical of these veterans was Dr. William Notson who spent three years with the Union army bandaging bullet wounds, amputating limbs and combating diseases including dysentery, typhoid fever and malaria. His exemplary service during the Battle of Gettysburg earned him a brevet promotion.[66]

Most of the fort's surgeons were commissioned officers serving as captains or lieutenants with the rank of "Assistant Surgeon." Each of these men passed a rigorous entrance examination designed to ensure that only well-trained and qualified applicants would serve in the department. Indeed, some of these men came from the finest medical schools in the country. Dr. Edwin Gardner, who enlisted as a private at the end of the Civil War, graduated from Harvard Medical School in 1875. Dr. William Corbusier studied medicine in California, served as surgeon in charge of the Sixth Illinois Cavalry during the war and completed his medical studies at Bellevue Hospital Medical College in New York City in 1867.[67]

When army physicians were unavailable, the medical department hired private citizens to serve the medical needs of the country's military posts. Mackinac Island physicians Drs. John R. Bailey and Hiram Mills worked as "Acting Assistant Surgeons" during this period. While Mills served only briefly in 1868, Dr. Bailey was hired on nine separate occasions between 1871 and 1895 to serve as fort physician. Bailey grew up at Fort Mackinac where his father, Dr. Joseph Bailey, was post surgeon in the 1850s. After receiving his medical degree from the University of Michigan, John Bailey established a private practice on Mackinac Island and made himself available to fort commanders who depended on his expertise during the frequent vacancies between army-assigned physicians. For Bailey, working at the fort – which earned him two dollars for every visit in 1889 – provided a welcome supplement to his regular income.[68] Dr. Harlan McVay began his career at Fort Mackinac as a civilian physician earning one-hundred dollars per month after completing his studies at Miami University (Ohio) Medical School. While at Fort Mackinac he passed the army medical examination in New York City in October 1889 and received his commission as assistant surgeon a few weeks later.[69]

Commissioned Officers – Duties and Responsibilities

Commissioned officers supervised all aspects of garrison life at Fort Mackinac from preparing their men for battle to regulating the use of the flush toilets. Under the direction of the commandant, officers cared for buildings, grounds and equipment, ordered and distributed food, uniforms and supplies, supervised assembly, inspection and drill, administered military justice and nursed sick and injured soldiers back to health. All of this and much more was meticulously documented with a never-ending flow of paperwork to regimental, departmental, division and army headquarters.

Fort Mackinac's commandant, appointed by the regimental commander, was the post's highest ranking officer and the ultimate authority. His day was filled with a wide variety of administrative, supervisory and public relations responsibilities.

The commandant's primary responsibility was to assign and oversee the work of his officers who in turn ran the daily affairs of the post. In carrying out this responsibility commandants demonstrated a variety of management styles while working with their subordinate officers. Captain Leslie Smith was a controlling, detail-orientated officer. When he took command in May 1869, Smith immediately established times for the daily duty calls, assigned administrative tasks to his lieutenants and convened boards of survey to audit the post treasurer's accounts, examine the condition of the buildings and report on the number of uniforms in storage. Particularly concerned about fire,

Captain Leslie Smith, photographed while serving as Fort Mackinac commander in the early 1870s.

Smith banned smoking in several buildings, ordered inspections of every wood stove and chimney and insisted that new stove installations be approved by an officer before being used. Over the next few months Smith fired a laundress, specified the size of rifle range targets, determined the distribution of garden vegetables and ordered his men to capture and kill all dogs running loose in the garrison.[70]

Smith remained very much in control during five years in command at Fort Mackinac, sometimes to the consternation of his officers, particularly his surgeons. Unable to keep tabs on Dr. Notson, Smith accused his medical officer of spending too much time at the Mission House and at a "low grog shop" in the village, thereby neglecting his duties at the fort. Notson fired off a barrage of counter charges claiming that Smith misused government property for his own benefit. Smith responded with a series of petty orders designed to assert his authority including insisting that Notson use his full signature on all official correspondence instead of just using his "surname only, in imitation of German Counts."[71] The power struggle continued with Notson's successor Dr. Carlos Carvallo who wanted to add a window to the post guardhouse to improve ventilation for the prisoners. Smith rejected Carvallo's request and responded that, if anything, the prison cell should be made less comfortable so that men would "not be so anxious to get in confinement."[72]

Captain Smith's controlling nature also affected his relationship with island residents. In March 1870 he ordered five village saloon keepers to stop selling liquor to his men, a move probably contemplated

Dr. William Notson.

but never seriously considered by other commanders. Smith even went so far as to threaten legal action should they fail to comply with his order.[73] Smith's boldest and certainly most unpopular move occurred two months later when he sent an armed detail to close the village school, housed in the former Indian Dormitory. Irritated by the "bad conduct of the children" who were climbing over the fence into the military reserve during recess and "hurling stones down the hill," Smith received permission to transfer the government-owned building to the war department. Villagers were incensed by the commandant's use of armed soldiers to evacuate their children.

LEIB IMAGE ARCHIVES

Mustering their legal and political forces, local leaders ultimately triumphed when an act of Congress turned the property over to the island board of education several weeks later.[74]

In contrast to Captain Smith was his predecessor Captain John Mitchell. Mitchell, perhaps as a result of his multiple war wounds and chronic alcoholism, neglected key responsibilities. He ignored the care and upkeep of several buildings especially the post chapel which was "completely gutted" and had the appearance of being "sacked by an invading army" and another building which was "shamefully abused" by an illegal post trader. Mitchell also left his successor with incomplete paperwork and poorly managed projects.[75]

Most commanders fell somewhere between Smith and Mitchell. Once a year a staff officer from the inspector general's office evaluated the condition and management of the post. Fort Mackinac commandants fared well under these inspections. In general, inspectors reported that they maintained firm control over their men and carefully managed the facilities. Most, like Captain George Brady, were efficient and fair in enforcing regulations and their soldiers were "well and judiciously commanded."[76]

Beginning in 1875 the Fort Mackinac commandant became superintendent of Mackinac National Park and received a new and diverse set of tasks. The legislation creating the national park established a series of rules and regulations that the commandant had to enforce. He soon had his soldiers patrolling the park to keep tourists from stripping bark from birch trees and to break up "confidence games and arrest three card monte men."[77] Commandants also contracted with local builders and supervised park construction projects including new stairways, fences and roads. The most time-consuming new duty was overseeing park property on which lessees built summer cottages. The commandant administered a never-ending flow of correspondence dealing with lease forms and payments, letters of recommendation, building plans and construction timetables.

Company officers supported the commandant in running the post. They assisted with the daily administration of the fort and held positions of specific responsibility. The officer of the day was in charge of the guard, prisoners and police of the garrison. He inspected the buildings and grounds, had overall responsibility for the daily operations in the fort and was expected to visit the guard posts throughout the night – probably the least favorite task of the officer of the day. In December 1882 Captain Edwin Sellers reprimanded Lieutenant Dwight Kelton for consistently failing to visit the guard after midnight during his tours as officer of the day. Further, Sellers scolded, "The commanding officers should not be obliged to call the attention of any officer of this post to this fact." Officers worked as quartermaster, commissary of subsistence, post treasurer, signal officer, ordnance officer, post canteen officer, target range officer and officer in charge of the post school. The post adjutant served as administrative assistant to the commandant responsible for correspondence, daily orders and maintaining company books and records. Commandants usually assigned each officer multiple tasks and rotated responsibilities to fairly distribute the work load.

Leslie Avenue winds through Mackinac Island's scenic forest. The road was cut in 1889 by command of Captain Greenleaf A. Goodale and named in honor of former commandant Leslie Smith.

Officers, including post surgeons, spent a considerable amount of time on court martial duty. Garrison courts martial, requiring the services of four officers, were frequently held to try men accused of petty crimes. Although less frequent, general courts martial trials for more serious crimes required at least six officers and frequently involved travel to other Great Lakes posts.

Along with general courts martial assignments, officers left the post on other "detached duty" tasks. In 1868 Edwin Gaskill spent nearly eight months assigned to the "Bureau of Freedman and Abandoned Lands" office in Washington, D.C. His work in the Bureau, set up by the War Department in 1865, was to assist with Civil War relief activities relating to refugees and freedmen. Officers on recruiting service usually left the fort for an extended period of time. Charles Davis was gone for two years in the early 1880s and Calvin Cowles spent nearly three years recruiting soldiers in New York City before returning to his company at Fort Mackinac. Other officers were detached for educational purposes. Bogardus Eldridge spent two years as professor of military science and tactics at Maryland Agricultural College while George Davis attended classes at the Infantry and Cavalry School at Fort Leavenworth, Kansas in 1889. Of shorter duration were the convict escort duties given to officers. Lieutenant John M. Webster spent four days delivering Private John Hanrahan to a Columbus, Ohio prison after he was convicted by a general court martial in 1875. George Davis escorted Thomas Conroy and David Evans to the Fort Leavenworth penitentiary in June 1888 and returned to the Kansas prison six months later with Henry Pedigrew and Frank Darlington.[79]

For all of these tasks, along with daily roll call, weekly inspections, dress parade, company drill and a myriad of other military duties, officers received a monthly salary significantly higher than the enlisted man. Newly commissioned second lieutenants in the infantry earned $1,400 a year, about nine times the salary of a first year private. First lieutenants earned $1,500, captains $1,800 and majors $2,500. Assistant surgeons began at a first lieutenant's wage level and were entitled to captain's pay after five years of service. Although modest by comparison to the salaries of other professionals, an officer's income also included free housing, heating fuel and a food allowance equaling ten percent of their salary. These salaries remained unchanged from 1870 to 1898. The only raise an officer at Fort Mackinac could look forward to was his "fogy," a ten-percent longevity pay increase given every five years.

An officer had to carefully budget his expenses, especially if he was raising a family. Early in his military career Calvin Cowles realized that money would be tight and his family finances "nip and tuck." As his children grew Cowles became increasingly concerned about their future needs, especially in the event of his untimely death. Before facing hostile forces in the Uncompahgre Ute Campaign in 1880, Cowles took stock of his financial resources and asked his father to manage his estate should he be killed. His meager death benefits included a single payment of $1,500 to his wife Mary from the Army Mutual Aid Association and a government survivor's pension of seventeen dollars per month, plus two dollars for each child. He also had about $100 in cash and loan notes worth about $300. Calvin also asked his father to care for his family, ensuring him that Mary was "very economical and will adapt herself to circumstances."[80]

Cowles expressed a common concern when he wrote in 1883: "Army officers are generally lucky if they are not in debt. I manage by great economy to keep even and

that is about all. I don't know what I will
do when the children grow up and have to
go to school." In an effort to avoid a string
of debts, Cowles ascribed to the principle
"economise and pay as you go." It must
have been particularly embarrassing when
he had to borrow money to complete his
move from New York to Mackinac in 1887.
Cowles, having miscalculated his travel-
ling expenses "on account of the interstate
law," was stranded in Detroit until a quick
loan from friends paid for his train ride to
Mackinac.[81]

While senior officers regularly evaluated subordinates, the process was informal
and had little impact on career advancement. All promotions for commissioned
officers were based strictly on seniority until
1890 when Congress required officers
below the rank of major to pass comprehensive written and physical examinations
to qualify for promotion. In the same year,

FORT VERDE STATE HISTORIC PARK

West Point cadet graduation photograph of Calvin D. Cowles, 1873.

senior officers began issuing "efficiency reports" on subordinates. Although these
reports were not used in the promotion process initially, they provided a permanent
record of professional evaluation, documented the problems of incompetent officers
and identified talented individuals for specific assignments.[82] In 1894 Fort Mackinac
commandant Major Clarence Bennett used the efficiency report to describe thirty-
three year veteran Captain Charles Witherell as a "successful company commander"
adding, "He has an excellent company, one of the best evidences of zeal and ability
in performance of military duty." Not all reports were so complimentary. In 1890
Colonel Henry Mizner remarked that Captain Thomas Sharpe "should be retired for
inefficiency." Sharpe, who served at Fort Mackinac in the early 1870s, continued to
receive unfavorable reports over the next few years and in 1895 the reviewing officer
concluded that he was not qualified mentally, morally or physically for the duties of
his position. Further, his capacity for command was "Not good, for want of faculty
and aptitude."[83] Sharpe finally retired from the service three years later.

Although officers and enlisted men served in the same company, there was a very
real and meaningful divide between the two in the late nineteenth century. Officers
gave commands and enlisted men carried them out. There was little, if any, frater-
nization on the job. Officers tended to work together in the post headquarters and communicated with their men through non-commissioned officers. Socially, officers and
enlisted men traveled in entirely different circles and rarely mingled outside the fort.

Despite their obviously different stations, Fort Mackinac's officers and enlisted men occasionally enjoyed a sense of camaraderie, especially when they shared mutual athletic interests. In 1885 Lieutenant Edward Pratt helped organize the fort baseball team by serving as team captain and second basemen. Mifflin Brady, son of the post commander played right field, but enlisted men comprised the rest of the team. This squad played several games on the island and traveled to nearby northern Michigan communities for their away games. Similarly, Pratt and other officers belonged to the fort's recreational rifle team that included nine enlisted men and competed against area teams.[84]

These and other opportunities tended to moderate the chasm between officer and enlisted men. So too did the mutual respect that sometimes resulted from years of shared service especially if it included battlefield experiences. It was not uncommon for officers to have deep respect and admiration for long-serving and faithful soldiers. Many enlisted men revered officers who demonstrated leadership skills and treated their troops with evenhanded respect. Still the unofficial caste system meant that officers and enlisted men, while occupying the same fort, lived in two very different worlds.

Members of the Fort Mackinac rifle club pose with the silver trophy they won in a contest with the Cheboygan Gun club in 1886. Lieutenant Edward Pratt is standing, third from left.

Chapter IV

The Daily Routine

ORT MACKINAC SOLDIERS lived a very structured life based on a daily routine that began at dawn and continued throughout the day. The post hummed with activity as soldiers responded to the duty calls of bugle, drum and fife. Recruits drilled on the parade ground, guards mounted sentry beats, an armed squad marched to the rifle range, a closely-guarded group of prisoners performed hard labor, medical staff attended sick soldiers, gardeners cultivated rows of vegetables and officers processed reams of paperwork. These, and dozens of other tasks, were accomplished every day in order to keep the garrison running smoothly.

Each day at Fort Mackinac, except Sundays and holidays, began the same way – with the sound of bugle and drum announcing the new day and serving as an alarm clock for the soldiers. On November 6, 1879 the men of Companies C and D, Tenth Infantry rolled out of their bunks at 6:15 a.m. to the sound of "First Call." Captain Seller's new winter schedule was in effect and the soldiers appreciated the extra half hour of sleep as they dressed and assembled on the parade. As part of the morning ceremony soldiers raised the flag, first sergeants shuffled men into formation in front of the barracks and the officer of the day took the roll call. The rest of their winter days would be ordered by the same schedule of daily signals. Throughout the period 1867-1895 soldiers followed a similar daily routine with minor seasonal variations.[85]

```
1st Call for Reveille . . . . . . . 6:15 a.m.
Reveille . . . . . . . . . . . . . . . 6:25 a.m.
Assembly . . . . . . . . . . . . . . 6:30 a.m.
Breakfast Call. . . . . . . . . . . 6:45 a.m.
Sick Call. . . . . . . . . . . . . . . 7:30 a.m.
Fatigue Call . . . . . . . . . . . . 7:45 a.m.
School Call . . . . . . . . . . . . 8:50 a.m.
1st Call-Guard mounting . . . 9:20 a.m.
Guard mounting. . . . . . . . . . 9:30 a.m.
1st Sergeant's Call . . . . . . . 11:00 a.m.
Recall from fatigue. . . . . . . 11:30 a.m.
Dinner Call . . . . . . . . . . . 11:45 a.m.
1st Call. . . . . . . . . . . . . . . 12:50 p.m.
Drill Call . . . . . . . . . . . . . 1:00 p.m.
Fatigue Call . . . . . . . . . . . . 1:00 p.m.
Recall from drill. . . . . . . . . 1:45 p.m.
Recall from fatigue. . . . . . . 4:15 p.m.
1st Call-Retreat . . . . . . . . . 10 minutes before sunset
Retreat . . . . . . . . . . . . . . . Sunset
School Call,  . . . . . . . . . . . Mondays, Wednesdays, Fridays
                                    – immediately after Retreat
Tattoo 1st Call . . . . . . . . . . 8:15 p.m.
Assembly . . . . . . . . . . . . . 8:25 p.m.
Tattoo. . . . . . . . . . . . . . . . 8:30 p.m.
Taps . . . . . . . . . . . . . . . . . 9:30 p.m.
1st Call-Sunday Inspection . . 9:20 a.m.
Sunday Inspection . . . . . . . . 9:30 a.m.
```

After roll call the men returned to their barracks squad rooms, passed through the wash room and headed into the mess hall at the back of the building. Heavy china serving plates filled with piping hot food awaited them on long tables flanked with low benches, a testimony to the work of the company cooks that began several hours earlier. Breakfast was the soldiers' second largest meal of the day and usually consisted of a meat dish, bread and coffee. On January 15, 1875 the men of Company E, Twenty-second Infantry awoke to a breakfast of fried bacon, fresh bread, coffee and sugar. The breakfast menu changed little over the next ten months except that the bacon was sometimes boiled rather than fried. Two years later the soldiers enjoyed a little more variety in their morning meal with main dishes of beef hash with potatoes and onions, corn meal mush with molasses, and fish and potato hash.[86]

After breakfast, the post surgeon addressed the garrison's medical needs at "Sick Call." Soldiers seeking medical attention trudged up to the post hospital just outside the east wall of the fort. The spacious building included an office/dispensary, where the surgeon examined soldiers, a store room, kitchen and quarters for the matrons and stewards on the first floor and three sick ward rooms with ten beds on the second floor. Additional space became available in 1887 when the adjacent stewards' quarters was constructed. Just behind the hospital a "deadhouse" (morgue) was added in 1890 and a nearby shed housed the hospital's "red cross ambulance."[87] Upon assuming charge of the hospital in 1874, Dr. J. V. DeHanne was generally pleased with the condition of the building. He found a full supply of medicines, obstetrical and dental tools and a "meagre supply of inferior surgical instruments." DeHanne was likewise pleased with the hospital library which contained several useful books and an extensive list of current medical journals, a particularly valuable resource for physicians so far away from professional support.[88]

While Mackinac was generally considered a healthy post, various illnesses and accidents tested the skills of the medical officers. Between 1885 and 1894 fort surgeons treated 822 cases, 650 for disease and 172 for injuries. The combined loss to the army was 5,633 days of service. In each case the physician had to determine if the

Fort Mackinac's post hospital with the upper gun platform in the foreground.

patient was to be admitted to the hospital, restricted to quarters or sent back to duty. Post surgeons cared for 471 soldiers in the hospital while 351 men were treated in their quarters. The most common diseases were influenza (104 cases) bronchial and respiratory ailments (92), stomach and intestinal disorders (78), rheumatism (56) and headache and neuralgia (41). Behavioral related diseases also took a toll on the garrison, much to the dismay of the post commandant. There were sixty cases of alcoholism and thirty-nine men treated for venereal disease, primarily gonorrhea and syphilis. Men were also treated for various other illnesses from insanity and epilepsy to boils, bunions, scabies and warts.[89]

Surgeons became particularly concerned when illnesses reached epidemic levels. After treating numerous cases of stomach and bowel disease in August 1887, Dr. Charles Woodruff traced the problem to the town drinking water. Because the fort pumping engine was broken, the garrison was drawing its water directly from the harbor using the village pump. To his horror, Woodruff discovered that this area near the main dock was polluted with refuse and sewage from village stores and nearby vessels. Based on Woodruff's recommendation, Captain Goodale instructed the men to draw water from the spring below the fort with the water cart until the pump could be fixed.[90]

An influenza epidemic put forty-four men on sick report in January 1890. Although Dr. Harlan McVay did not discover the source he did observe that the disease began with Company K in the first floor squad room of the soldiers barracks and spread to the men of Company E on the upper floor about a week later. When a second influenza epidemic hit the fort a year later and progressed through the barracks in the same manner, Dr. McVay concluded that the building was partially to blame. The "unfavorable location, inferior means of ventilation and faulty construction" of the lower quarters, he argued, was "in great measure responsible for the severity of the disease in that company." Despite McVay's complaints about the unhealthiness of this squad room, which echoed comments made by medical staff since the early 1870s, nothing was done to alleviate the problem.[91]

Post surgeons treated soldiers for injuries including contusions and sprains, wounds and lacerations, fractures and dislocations, frostbite and burns. Most were minor injuries that required little attention beyond the initial treatment. Such was the case when Dr. Bailey treated and released four men who suffered from frostbite in the frigid winter of 1885 when sub-zero temperature readings were common. A more serious injury tested Dr. Bailey's surgical skills one year later when winter claimed another victim. Private Peter Mitchell dislocated his left forearm at the elbow when he fell from a roof while shoveling snow. Within an hour Dr. Bailey had reduced the dislocation while Mitchell was sedated with a "chloroform anesthesia."[92]

While most injuries occurred in the line of duty, post surgeons also saw an interesting variety of "recreational" wounds. In May 1887 Dr. Bailey treated several soldiers who were injured while playing baseball. After setting a dislocated finger, wrapping a sprained ankle and bandaging a lacerated thumb, Bailey commented that the "mod-

The post cemetery, nestled in a shady stand of mature oak, maple and pine trees, was the military burying ground from the 1820s until the fort was abandoned in 1895.

ern way of playing baseball appears to result in 'Cruelty to Animals.'" He added, "The game is manly and commendable but less objectionable methods of playing could be devised; it should not be brutal."[93] Four months later Dr. Woodruff attended to the wounds of Private Martin Curley who was "bitten in a drunken brawl in a rum-shop." Curley, perhaps to avoid the condemnation of Dr. Woodruff, sought treatment from village druggist Mr. Bogan who applied a "court plaster" to the wound. Curley was compelled to see Woodruff at sick call two days later after the wound became seriously infected. Furious, Woodruff fired off a series of letters to store owner M. G. Bailey accusing Bogan of malpractice and demanding that he stop treating soldiers. Bailey shot back that he would continue serving soldiers claiming that, "If a drug store can't sell court plaster it had better close up especially if you consider them responsible for a drunken man's acts or doctor's mistakes."[94]

Enlisted men incapacitated by illnesses or injuries were usually discharged from the army with a surgeon's certificate of disability. Between 1885 to 1894 only fourteen men received a medical discharge because of illness or injury including Peter Mitchell who was permanently disabled because of his elbow injury and discharged six months after the accident. By contrast, forty-one men of Company B, Forty-third Infantry (1867-1869), representing more than seventy percent of the company, received disability discharges. This company of soldiers, all wounded Civil War Veterans, was barely up to the task of caring for a peaceful post like Fort Mackinac and would have been of little use in combat or on duty in a rugged western outpost.

Twelve soldiers died at Fort Mackinac during this period as a result of illness or injury. Dr. George Adair began treating Sergeant John McGrath in the fall of 1880 for acute bronchitis. Adair attributed McGrath's illness to his quartermaster responsibilities which required him to walk up and down the fort hill as often as twenty times a day, sometimes in cold and inclement weather. For the next several months McGrath was in and out of the post hospital receiving treatment as his heart and lungs began to fail. During the last month he stayed in his quarters in town where he suffered greatly until he died on March 15, 1881. His funeral took place two days later at Ste. Anne's Church and he was buried in the island's Roman Catholic cemetery. Similarly, Private Alvin Bates endured a long illness before he died. Bates arrived at Fort Mackinac in December 1873 already suffering from an "intermittent fever" for which he was treated at Fort Wayne, Detroit. Bates' condition grew steadily worse and in May Dr. Carvallo diagnosed him with typhoid fever. Over the next month Bates weakened, contracted pneumonia and died on June 13, 1874.[96]

Pneumonia also claimed the life of Captain Edwin Sellers. Unlike McGrath and Bates, Sellers' illness was short and his death sudden. During a spring thaw Sellers opened the cellar beneath his quarters to take stock of his remaining food supplies. While sweating as he worked in the cramped space the post commander took off his uniform coat and subsequently became chilled. Within a few days he contracted pneumonia and after a short illness died on April 8, 1884. The forty-four year old Sellers left a wife and three young sons. Fanny Corbusier, wife of the post surgeon who attended Sellers, reported that "nearly the whole population of the island" attended Sellers' funeral and interment in the post cemetery four days

Edwin Sellers, Fort Mackinac post commandant from 1879 until his death in 1884.

later. Upon assuming command of the post, Captain Charles Davis expressed the sentiments of the entire garrison community when he wrote of the popular commandant: "We all loved him and there will ever remain in the hearts of his friends a recollection of his manly worth, earnest devotion to duty, fidelity in friendship and generous sympathies that will serve to keep his memory cherished so long as one remains."

In honor of their fallen captain, the officers and men of Fort Mackinac wore the "usual badge of mourning," a black crepe band on their left arm and swords, for the next thirty days.[97]

Only two Fort Mackinac soldiers during this period died as a result of accident.

Andrew Simonson, a twenty-six year old Norwegian-born private, was killed by the premature discharge of a cannon he was firing during a national salute on July 4, 1870. Hospital Steward Judson Rogers drowned in Lake Michigan near Charlevoix when the steamer *Champlain* burned and sank on June 17, 1887. Accompanied by his six-year-old son Leon, Rogers was returning from having dental work done in Milwaukee. Father and son became separated when the boat sank and while Judson's body was soon discovered Leon remained lost at sea. Charlevoix officials sent a telegram to Fort Mackinac after finding a note in Judson's pocket reading, "If anything happens to me write my wife Mrs. J. J. Rogers, Fort Mackinac, Mich."[98] Anna Rogers, a matron in the fort hospital, buried her husband on June 19. Five days later Leon's body was discovered at the head of Little Traverse Bay. The next day, following services at Ste. Anne's Church, Anna reunited her husband and son on the south side of the post cemetery.

When not treating sick or injured soldiers, surgeons spent considerable time inspecting garrison facilities and recommending sanitary changes. At military posts throughout the country surgeons took the lead at combating disease arising from sanitary conditions. As a result, Fort Mackinac's surgeons inspected and commented on a wide range of sanitation issues such as drainage, refuse disposal, water supply, heating systems, food quality and preparation and soldiers' personal hygiene.

A surgeon's passion in the area of military hygiene often put him at odds with the commandant and the post guardhouse was a frequent source of conflict. As early as 1872, when Captain Leslie Smith and Dr. Carlos Carvallo battled over the ventilation problems in the prison cell, the guardhouse was a target of sanitation-minded surgeons. Two years later little had changed prompting Carvallo to comment, "It is to be regretted that the principles of public hygiene are not an obligatory study of all exercising command."[99] Carvallo's successors made little progress with guardhouse sanitation problems and by 1882 Dr. Bailey complained that a sentence in the prison cell exacerbated discipline problems:

> After inhaling the exhalations from human bodies all night, a prisoner is not in a fit condition the next morning to meditate on his misdemeanor or make good resolutions for the future, and if several be confined at one time for drunkenness the repeated inhalation of the fumes of alcohol from their breath will tend to prolong intoxication.[100]

Finally in the early 1880s, as a result of recommendations from Drs. Bailey and Corbusier, post commanders raised the ceiling, installed new stoves, constructed additional windows and added ventilation pipes to improve conditions in the prison cell.

Well-educated and with a thirst for knowledge, post surgeons occasionally engaged in special projects that were beyond the call of duty to pursue an interest or satisfy their intellectual curiosity. Dr. Carvallo filled the fort's medical journal with an overview of Mackinac history, a complete description of the fort and remarks on "the habits of *Coregonus albus* (white fish)." Working with Private Robert Wilson, Dr. Bailey gath-

23rd Infantry soldiers at the post guardhouse, ca. 1887.

ered daily temperature readings in the winter of 1885 to document the abnormally cold season. In looking for an explanation for the frigid weather, Bailey posited that "wholesale destruction of the forests of the two peninsulas of Michigan and adjacent territory, for fuel, mechanical purposes and cultivation of the soil, will, in some degree account for the low temperatures." Bailey, an avowed sports enthusiast, filled his journal with news of the fort's baseball and rifle teams including scores, rosters and schedules. Dr. McVay's interest turned to the natural wonders of Mackinac. With the assistance of Mrs. McVay, the post surgeon produced an exhaustive list of island flora in October 1891.[101]

§

While the ill and injured made their way to the hospital after "Sick Call," the rest of the command prepared for morning fatigue duty. Fort Mackinac, like most military installations, was self-contained and largely dependent on the skill and labor of its troops for upkeep and maintenance. This was accomplished through fatigue duty which included a wide range of daily and special tasks: construction, repair and painting of walls, ramparts, quarters and storehouses; hauling away trash, refuse and kitchen slops; repair of tools, wagons and equipment; planting, cultivating and harvesting the company gardens; feeding, grooming and shoeing horses and mules; stacking firewood, hauling coal, policing the grounds, filling the ice house and dozens of other garrison chores.

Most soldiers tackled fatigue chores as a part of daily duty assignments, but for those earning extra duty pay these special tasks provided a great opportunity to pad their paycheck. Private Amos Wilkie, a twenty-five year old house painter who joined the army in 1886, earned extra duty pay plying his trade in 1888. Wilkie spent

Private Amos Wilkie.

the summer months (when he was not in jail for being absent without leave) painting buildings around the parade ground brown. Captain Goodale ordered the change to provide "a great relief to the eyes" because of the glare from the white buildings and gravel parade ground.[102] Thomas Hennessey was a very successful first sergeant with Company E Twenty-third Infantry in the 1880s. After he was discharged in Texas in August 1890 he longed to return to Mackinac Island and joined Company C Nineteenth Infantry as a private one month later. Hennessey made up for his salary loss by spending most of the next three years on extra duty as a plumber in the quartermaster's department earning an extra thirty-five cents a day. Like Wilkie and Hennessey, soldiers with special skills, including masons, carpenters, teamsters, blacksmiths and others, were able to supplement their income while on fatigue duty.

For those not earning extra money, fatigue duty was often the most onerous part of their day. Hours of lifting heavy stones, shoveling latrine pits through rocky soil and filling wheelbarrows with kitchen waste was enough to discourage most soldiers. For those who expected swashbuckling excitement when they joined the army, fatigue duty was certainly a disappointment. Fed up with fatigue duty on July 7, 1887, Private Harry Fagan snuck off, got a bottle of liquor and headed to the woods were he was found "in a drunken or stupid condition" a few hours later. Fagan paid a ten-dollar fine after he was found guilty by court martial.[103] A few months earlier Sergeant Charles Hastings was charged with being absent from ice cutting detail. After receiving permission to "go to the rear" (relieve himself), Hastings failed to return and was found in a saloon where he was arrested by Quartermaster Sergeant John Fletcher. The smooth-talking sergeant was able to convince officers at his subsequent court martial trial that he had a good reason for being in the bar and he was acquitted. A month later Hastings was promoted to first sergeant.[104]

§

On November 6, 1879 while most of his company mates were plugging away at fatigue duty, Sergeant John Devlin was busy preparing to teach class in the post school-house. Thirteen years earlier Congress passed legislation requiring the army to maintain school facilities for the education of enlisted men at all permanent posts. The legislation lacked strategies for carrying out this broad mission and little was done at most garrisons until 1878. In General Order No. 24 the army again instructed officers to provide educational opportunities for soldiers, but this time Congress provided the funds needed for constructing schoolhouses. A year later Fort Mackinac's schoolhouse was built and in June 1879 Sergeant Devlin was appointed Overseer of Schools. During the day Devlin taught the children of the garrison with three nights a week scheduled for the instruction of enlisted men.[105]

Lieutenant John Webster supervised Devlin and established the first course of studies and list of rules for the Fort Mackinac schoolhouse. Webster chose text books and established a schedule of instruction starting at 6:30 p.m. with writing followed by arithmetic, spelling and reading and concluding with a twenty-minute course on "history and writing" at 8:40 p.m. Soldiers were instructed to be neat and orderly in appearance and warned that talking, loud whispering and unnecessary noise, along with tobacco chewing, were prohibited. Webster issued text books including Davis' *Arithmetic* and William Swinton's *Condensed School History of The United States* and encouraged his men to take them to their squad rooms for further study.[106]

The army's educational efforts provided mixed results in the late nineteenth century. While congressional funds made possible the construction of many new schools, there were still thirty-eight posts without educational facilities in 1881. Other posts lacked proper textbooks and many could not find competent teachers. These were not issues at Fort Mackinac which enjoyed a new schoolhouse, adequate supplies and skilled teachers (Sergeant Devlin remained in charge of the school for over two years and his successor, Sergeant Frederick J. Grant – the "good French Scholar," taught school for nearly a year and a half.) The biggest issue at the Fort Mackinac school, and throughout the army, was that education programs were not compulsory.

Voluntary school attendance, combined with other mandatory assignments (especially guard duty) resulted in low and irregular use of the school by enlisted men. In January 1883 Sergeant Grant's class averaged seven pupils. Commandant Sellers was pleased with the progress he saw: "A number of the men state that they have derived material benefits from attending the school; the elementary branches were taught, each man selecting such studies as he desired to learn." But attendance remained modest and, as the weather warmed, class size shrunk until Grant was without any students in June. Despite the occasional flurry of educational activity, school attendance remained weak. In 1885 Captain George Brady summarized the problem at Fort Mackinac and across the country, "Until attendance of Post Schools be made mandatory, I do not think they will be successful and the money appropriated for a school teacher at this post would be put to better use."[107]

The army addressed the problem with General Order No. 9 in January 1889 when it required soldiers needing education to attend classes. Because school was now part of military duty, classes were held during the day. At Fort Mackinac, Captain Goodale immediately established a daily hour-long school program beginning at 1:00 p.m. and allowed his company commanders to select appropriate students. Attendance was obligatory and only those who were sick, on guard duty or confined in the guardhouse were excused. The order had the desired effect and by July Goodale proudly reported that he had twenty pupils regularly attending classes.[108]

The army mandated educational programs for officers beginning in 1891. Commanding General John M. Schofield ordered lyceums established at each post so that officers could share information with each other on a regular basis. In response to the order, Major Edwin Coates inaugurated the Fort Mackinac Officers Lyceum on November 3, 1891. The officers decided to meet twice a week at 10:00 a.m. with Tuesday meetings devoted to the study of military law and Thursday meetings concentrating on infantry drill regulation. The officers quickly abandoned the idea of studying military law and spent the next nine sessions reviewing and discussing individual paragraphs of the drill manual. The presentations became infinitely more interesting when the officers began presenting their own papers. On January 21, 1892 Lieutenant Joseph Frazier delivered a talk on "Amusement and Recreation of Enlisted Men" and two weeks later Lieutenant Henry Leanard spoke on "The Summary Court." Fort Mackinac's Post Lyceum continued to meet every year from November through April until the garrison was reduced in 1894.[109]

§

While educational programs were a phenomenon of the army's late nineteenth century reform movement, guard duty was a daily task that soldiers had been doing for centuries. Men on guard duty provided security to the garrison by patrolling the fort walls, watching over prisoners and keeping a lookout for fires. At 9:20 a.m. on November 6, 1879 the Fort Mackinac musicians sounded first call for guard duty. Ten minutes later a squad of soldiers dressed in clean uniforms with polished shoes and sparkling rifles stood at attention on the parade ground in front of the guardhouse. The sergeant of the new guard inspected his men making sure they were ready for duty. Across from them the old guard assembled and, upon the order of the officer of the day, the guard was changed and another twenty-four hour vigil began. This simple but formal ceremony took place every morning, every day of the year.

The guard usually consisted of between six and ten men, depending on the number of available privates. On May 18, 1883 one sergeant, one corporal and

Sentries on duty at post number one near the guardhouse, ca. 1890.

five privates from Companies C and D, Tenth Infantry mounted guard. With a total of thirty privates available for guard duty that May, the men could expect a six day guard rotation or, roughly, one guard duty stint per week.[110]

Men on guard duty rotated between the sentry beats and the guardhouse. The number of sentries varied but there was always at least one man on duty at post number one, the parapet above the south sally port. Sentinels wore undress uniforms, belts and cartridge boxes and carried rifles at all times. They stopped and challenged all who approached their post at night, requiring the daily password for anyone who wanted to enter the fort. Every hour they called out the number of their post and "All is well." Sentinels were never to leave their beat and allowed to use the sentry boxes only in inclement weather. When Private John Lambert was found asleep in his sentry box on a warm, dry July evening in 1879 he was arrested and confined. The fort officers sent a clear message about the importance of remaining vigilant while on guard duty when they found Lambert guilty of quitting his post and confined him at hard labor for three months.[111]

While Lambert spent his guard duty sleeping, others kept awake day dreaming about baseball games, their next visit to the village or women. Sergeant William Fenley used the quiet hours of a late June night in 1888 to write a poem to his girlfriend Mary Eva Toohey who lived in the village below the fort. From his perch high above the town the Irish-born sergeant kept a careful watch over Mary's house when he wrote,

'Tis late – advanced is the night;
A sentinel am I,
And beat my post left and right
Beneath a starry sky:
From my lofty post all around
I watch and listen to every sound.

I watch the dwellings in the Fort,
And in the village below;
If danger happens I report
The alarm bugle to blow.
Above all, that spot I watch,
Where sleeps my darling in her virgin
  couch.

I watch each shining, twinkling star
In the blue expanse above,
And in the solemn silence near and far,
I pray for my Mary love:
May He who know no sleep or slumber
Watch over my Mary years without
  number.

Sergeant William Fenley and
Mary Eva Toohey.

Sentinels were relieved every two hours (sometimes more often in very cold weather) and allowed to return to the guardhouse although they could not remove any part of their clothing or accoutrements. Soldiers stationed in the guardhouse ate, slept and played cards but also kept watch over prisoners in the jail cell. Men awaiting trial or serving court martial sentences often worked on cleanup or hard labor tasks during the day and returned to the cell at night. During the evening guards kept a close eye on prisoners, making sure that they remained behind bars; failure to do so resulted in severe and speedy punishment. On March 14, 1886 William Williams, while serving as sergeant of the guard, invited a prisoner to leave the cell and join him in a game of cards. When his misadventure was discovered by the officer of the day, Williams was arrested and thrown into the cell with his card-playing friend. Five days later a garrison court convicted Williams and reduced him to the rank of private.[112]

Misbehaving soldiers like Lambert and Williams were exceptions as most guards performed these tedious and repetitive duties with diligence. At 8:45 p.m. on November 4, 1888 Patrick Enright corporal of the guard was putting on his overcoat and heading out of the guardhouse door when he heard a commotion behind him. Sergeant George Robinson had rushed into the cell where he discovered two long-time trouble makers, privates Henry Pedigrew and Frank Darlington, receiving liquor by means of a rubber hose leading from outside through the barred window. Enright raced outside to the back of the building hoping to catch the conspiring soldier but only found an empty bottle – Duffy's Malt Whiskey – and a section of hose. The work done by Enright and Robinson in catching the men and collecting evidence was crucial to successful prosecution of the prisoners. Pedigrew and Darlington were dishonorably discharged from the army and sent to Leavenworth Prison where Darlington died of pneumonia four months later.[113]

At peaceful posts like Fort Mackinac fire, not enemy soldiers, was the greatest concern for patrolling sentinels. Although many Fort Mackinac buildings burned to the ground in earlier years, only the post bakery was lost to fire in the period 1867 to 1895. Village buildings were not so fortunate. Early in the morning of January 31, 1887 a fire engulfed Thomas Truscott's Saloon on Water Street (Main Street). The flames soon spread to several buildings in that crowded section of town including the Mackinac House, the Carson House, Murray's Store and the Chambers Building. The officers and men of the fort turned out at once and stopped the rapidly spreading fire by blowing up Preston's Empire Saloon. Bittersweet though it was for the enlisted men to see one of their favorite watering holes destroyed, the soldiers "prompt and energetic assistance" stopped the fire before it could do further damage.[114]

The tools for fighting fires evolved from "ladders and buckets" in 1872 to more sophisticated equipment in the 1890s which was made possible by the fort's modern plumbing system. After 1889, the fort was outfitted with nine seventy-gallon water tanks and three hydrants, one each at post headquarters, the sergeants quarters and laundresses quarters, to fight fires. Fortunately, the system was never used and no fort building was destroyed by fire after the post bakery burned to the ground in 1878.[115]

§

Fort musicians recalled soldiers from fatigue duty in late morning and sent them off to dinner, their largest meal of the day, fifteen minutes later. The soldier's daily

1870s soldier on guard duty at the south sally port. Note the water buckets for fire fighting on the bench to the far right.

ration included twenty ounces of beef, twelve of bacon and eighteen of bread along with beans, sugar, salt and coffee. The subsistence department calculated the rations needed for each post based on the number of men on the muster roll and shipped huge quantities of food to each post. At Fort Mackinac the food was received by the officer and sergeant in charge and stored in the Post Commissary with perishable foods going into the large, semi-subterranean cellar. Between 1870 and 1874 Fort Mackinac received 5,172 rations worth 22.46 cents each.[116] These numbers doubled after 1875 when the fort became a two-company post.

The actual meals served at Fort Mackinac during this period included other food that made the soldiers' dining experience considerably more enjoyable. Supplemental foods came from two sources: the company gardens and purchases. The land in front of Fort Mackinac served as the fort garden from the early years of occupation. Despite the short growing season in northern Michigan, this plot of land usually produced a

CLARKE HISTORICAL LIBRARY, CENTRAL MICHIGAN UNIVERSITY

Rows of vegetables fill the post garden in front of Fort Mackinac, ca. 1890.

bountiful crop of vegetables that greatly enhanced the soldiers' meals and provided necessary nutrition. Vegetables from the garden included beets, beans, onions, green corn, cabbage, lettuce, cucumbers, carrots, parsnips, peas, radishes, squash and rutabagas. Mackinac Island had a long-established reputation for producing delicious potatoes and soldiers grew them in great quantities. Fort gardeners had varying levels of success depending on the weather but 1885 was a bumper year with a yield of 710 bushels of potatoes, 225 of cabbage and 10 of onions.[117] Fort Mackinac soldiers rarely kept farm animals except for cows which provided the garrison with fresh milk.

Soldiers also purchased extra food with money from the company fund to add variety to the bland army ration. Company fund monies were raised by the sale of excess rations, particularly bread, meat and milk. In essence, the soldiers were trading part of their rations for more variety in their diet. Similarly, the post surgeon was able to sell some of the rations issued to his staff and patients. The proceeds from these sales were used to establish a hospital fund which was used, in part, to improve their meals. In 1892 the sale of extra rations and milk netted the hospital fund $110.80. Profits from the post canteen, also distributed to the company and hospital funds, provided the surgeon with an additional $55.76.[118]

With fresh vegetables from the garden and a steady cash flow to purchase extra food, soldiers at Fort Mackinac generally ate well. When the men of Company E, Twenty-second Infantry sat down for dinner on October 16, 1874 they enjoyed a hearty meal of roast beef, gravy, bread and vegetable soup with beans, peas, cabbage and carrots. When post canteen profits swelled the company fund beginning in 1889, soldiers purchased dinner treats including corn starch pudding, macaroni and cheese and stewed prunes. Throughout the period post surgeons were pleased to report that the food was healthy, the kitchens clean and the cooking satisfactory.[119]

The army provided a wide variety of foods for Fort Mackinac's company officers. Along with the enlisted men's rations these supplies were stored in the post commissary where officers and their wives shopped using their monthly food allowance. Officers' stores were notoriously expensive so families often bought their food in bulk at great savings. On November 13, 1883 Dr. Corbusier received his winter food supply from Detroit. He spent several hours packing a hind quarter of beef, whole lamb, half a barrel of corned beef, large keg of pickled pigs feet, salted fish, cabbages, potatoes, turnips, carrots, parsnips, sweet potatoes, onions, celery, apples and a barrel of cider into the cellar beneath his quarters. Just before Christmas Corbusier received his chickens, ducks and turkeys which were shipped to Mackinaw City by train and brought across the ice on horse drawn cart.[120]

Officers' dinners, usually prepared by hired servants, ran the gamut from quick meals to lavish feasts. One of the more sumptuous dinners was the "grand party" hosted by Dr. and Mrs. Carvallo in 1873 at their officers' stone quarters apartment. The twenty guests dined on turkey, chicken, duck, goose and oysters and drank multiple toasts with Dr. Carvallo's special "Russian Punch." The drink, mixed in a large bowl in the center of the table and consisting of various liquors and fruits, left a powerful impression on several guests including Kate Franks, who was carried "punch sick" into a back room, and "Mrs. W." who got turned around after rising for a toast and sat back down in a dish of chocolate ice cream. Those who were able to leave got home at six o'clock the next morning.[121]

Officers and enlisted men also purchased food from island merchants. George T. Arnold's merchandise store was a favorite shopping spot for fort soldiers. In the late 1880s seven officers and more than forty enlisted men maintained accounts at the store where they bought a wide variety of goods from cigars and shoestrings to envelopes and gloves. Food purchases included tomatoes (five pounds for thirty cents), fresh fish (eight and a half pounds for sixty cents) and special treats not available in the commissary including sardines, oysters and chocolate.[122] Several soldiers and their wives also purchased supplies at James Gallagher's grocery including Mary Manning, wife of Captain William Manning, who bought chickens, berries, cabbage and celery at the Water Street store.

§

After the mid-day meal many soldiers returned to fatigue duty while others drilled. Drill schedules at Fort Mackinac varied according to the interest and needs of the commanding officer. Captain John Mitchell, seeing little reason to put his wounded Civil War veterans through military exercises, rarely drilled his men more than once a day in the late 1860s. A few years later, however, Captain Leslie Smith drilled his raw recruits three times a day so that they could be ready for battle "with the least practicable delay." These young men must have questioned their decision to join the army when they learned that Smith's drills began at 6:00 o'clock in the morning.[123]

The purpose of all army drills was to sharpen soldiers' military skills. To this end Fort Mackinac's infantry soldiers practiced the manual of arms, bayonet exercise, marching, setting up exercises and facings. Although the fort cannons were fired nearly every day for the morning and evening salute, soldiers did not spend much time on artillery drill. One exception to this rule occurred on June 21, 1881 when Lieutenant Plummer was ordered to train a squad of twelve enlisted men on the fort cannons in

Soldiers at drill on the parade ground behind Fort Mackinac.

Soldier fires a daily salute from one of the upper gun platform cannons.

order to have "an expert and efficient detail" for the upcoming Fourth of July salute.[124]

Winter weather often restricted the drill schedule and limited the type of exercises. In December 1877 Major Hough's men conducted a full range of drills on the parade ground in good weather but practiced only the manual of arms in the barracks squad room when winter storms raged outside. Frustrated by these restrictions, Fort Mackinac officers frequently petitioned the army for a winter training facility. After watching his men stumble over foot lockers and scorch themselves on coal stoves, Captain Goodale requested permission to build a winter gymnasium. The War Department repeatedly denied his request, prompting the irritated captain to complain that his men constantly "visit the saloons and other resorts of the village" to avoid spending evenings in the same room "in which they have slept and drilled."[125]

Target practice with rifles received little attention in the years immediately after the Civil War until General Order No. 50 in 1869 established a renewed emphasis on marksmanship. In response to the order Captain Leslie Smith established a schedule of target practice at Fort Mackinac on September 22, 1869. Smith sent Lieutenant John Leonard and his soldiers to the range behind the fort where they fired their rifles at man-size targets at a range of 200 hundred yards. As an incentive to the enlisted men, Smith promised that the best shot at each practice would be excused from his next tour of guard duty. In a cost saving move, however, the army restricted soldiers to three shots apiece, hardly enough rounds to sharpen an infantryman's shooting skills.[126]

The army's tightfisted approach to target practice ammunition changed dramatically after the Battle of Little Bighorn in 1876. Custer's stunning defeat raised concerns about the rifle skills of United States soldiers and the army quickly increased the number of practice rounds to twenty shells per month. In the early 1880s a comprehensive system of target practice was developed by Colonel T. T. S. Laidley and installed at military posts around the country. Fort Mackinac officers soon realized that their 600 yard range behind the fort was too short for the Laidley system and a new 1000-yard range was built below the bluff east of Fort Holmes. The longer range was outfitted with a revolving Laidley target and a "Willard's telephone" to facilitate safe communication.[127]

Lieutenant Benjamin C. Morse oversees target practice at the island rifle range, 1890.

While the best season for target practice was summer, growing crowds of vacationers presented serious safety concerns for range officers. Captain George Brady considered abandoning summer target practice altogether in order to avoid "shooting some of the tourists who frequent the island." Brady's suggestion was impractical but the season was shortened in the late 1880s to mid-May through mid-July. The occasional summer regimental encampments, which brought hundreds of soldiers to the island from different Great Lakes forts, created additional safety concerns for the post commanders. Fort officers developed detailed safety procedures that were strictly enforced to protect both soldiers and visitors.[128]

The army established division and departmental rifle competitions that spurred officers and enlisted men alike to master the weapons. Target practice became the rage as men competed to represent their regiments and bring glory back to their companies. In 1885 post commandant George Brady proudly sent Captain Greenleaf Goodale, Corporal William Sconce and Private William Schwarzhoff to the annual rifle competition sponsored by the National Rifle Association at Creedmore, Long Island, New York. At the competition, in which army, militia and civilian sharp-

Fort Mackinac interpreters explain and demonstrate 1880s military rifles using original .45-70 "Trapdoor" Springfield rifles.

shooters competed, Corporal Sconce walked away with the prestigious Hilton Trophy Medal. Corporal William Williams joined Sconce in representing Fort Mackinac at army rifle competitions during the next few years and demonstrated remarkable talent with his "Trapdoor Springfield" rifle. Williams won the first place gold medal at the division championship at Fort Niagara in 1887 and, two years later, was selected for the army's elite group of "Distinguished Marksmen."[129]

Along with the military-sponsored competitions, Fort Mackinac soldiers also participated in rifle matches against civilian teams from neighboring towns. Several times during the mid-1880s Companies E and K, Twenty-third Infantry squared off against the Cheboygan Gun Club. The local team was usually no match for the boys in blue who won most matches including the contest held in Cheboygan on July 4, 1885. The fort team, led by Goodale, Sconce, Williams and Schwarzhoff, defeated the Cheboygan squad 401 to 385 and carried home a silver cup. A month later the two teams met again when the Cheboygan team traveled to the island. On their own rifle range the "Fort 10" once again bested their rivals and held on to the cup.[130]

Although target practice and military drills were of little use at peaceful posts, the training received at Fort Mackinac helped soldiers prepare for combat duty elsewhere. On Sunday July 9, 1876, just two weeks after Custer's defeat shocked the nation, Captain Charles Dickey received telegraphic orders to immediately join the "Terry Indian Expedition." Six days later Dickey and thirty-three men of Company E, Twenty-second Infantry left Fort Mackinac en route to Fort Abraham Lincoln, the same Dakota Territory fort from which Custer launched his ill-fated mission two months earlier. From there Dickey and his men marched to the Yellowstone River and joined General Alfred Terry's force on July 20, 1876. Nine days later they engaged the Indians at the mouth of the Powder River as a part of a larger offensive to push the Sioux and other tribes out of the Bighorn and Powder rivers region. After more than a year in the field, the battle-hardened men of Company E returned to Fort Mackinac.[131]

A much greater number of Fort Mackinac soldiers saw duty in the Spanish American War which began three years after the island post was abandoned. Dr. Woodruff and Captain Theodore Mosher served in Cuba during the war where Mosher was wounded in the battle of El Caney in 1898. Mosher recovered from his wounds and retired from service a year later. Other ex-Fort Mackinac officers were not so fortunate. Bogardus Eldridge and Edmund Smith were killed in action in the Philippine Islands. Another casualty was Woodbridge Geary, the officer who closed Fort Mackinac in 1895. Four years after leaving the peaceful shores of Mackinac Island Geary was severely wounded while leading troops on Luzon Island in the Philippines. Geary was transported to San Francisco where he eventually died of his

Edmund Smith, who served at Fort Mackinac in the early 1890s, died on February 5, 1900 from gunshot wounds received in action at Fort Amia, Philippine Islands.

wounds. Surgeons, too, became casualties of war. Dr. Harlan McVay, who a decade earlier was composing a list of wildflowers on Mackinac Island with his wife Flora, contracted typhoid fever and died in Manila on January 4, 1899.[132]

§

Recall from afternoon fatigue duty signaled the end of the soldier's work day. Tired from many hours of work, soldiers trudged back to their squad rooms and rested on their bunks, played a quick game of cards or attended to personal business. Supper call brought them once again to the mess hall where they ate their lightest meal of the day. In July 1876 supper consisted of bread, cheese, coffee and sugar. In the 1890s the well-fed men of the Nineteenth Infantry supped on hash, cold meats, stewed prunes and even baked fish along with the standard issue of bread and coffee.[133] Soldiers had free time after supper until the sound of Retreat at which time the flag was lowered, the evening salute fired and the men assembled on the parade ground for roll call. Later in the evening Tattoo was played and the men assembled for the final roll call of the day before being confined to quarters. Taps, usually played between 9:30 p.m. and 11:00 p.m. depending on the season, was the last call of the day and signaled lights out in the quarters. In the summer of 1887 Captain Goodale dispensed with the Tattoo roll call and allowed his men to stay out of their quarters until 11:00 p.m. Goodale repeated his generous offer the following summer until late August when a rash of misbehavior convinced him to revoke his order.[134]

Soldiers could apply for and receive passes to be absent from the post for the evening or even overnight. Passes were always in demand but especially so during the summer when the weather was pleasant, the days longer and the nights filled with activities. Most often soldiers on pass simply went to town for an evening in the saloon, a meal at one of the hotels or a party at the roller skating rink. Some traveled to St. Ignace, Cheboygan or Mackinaw City while others went fishing, hunting, sailing or skating. Groups of men sometimes received passes for special occasions. Eight enlisted men from the Tenth Infantry went to see a show in the village on August 6, 1883 and two weeks later a dozen men took an excursion to the Les Cheneaux Islands on board the *Messenger*.[135]

Officers insisted that their men represent the army in a positive and professional manner when on leave. Soldiers were required to be in proper military dress and respect the time restrictions on their passes. In 1875 Captain Dickey allowed his men to wear their five-button blouses into town except on Sundays when the dress uniform was required. Nine years later Captain Brady ordered his men on pass to enter and exit through the south sally port and surrender their passes at the guardhouse when they returned. He further warned that "anyone returning in a demoralized condition, or who has behaved badly, will be deprived of such indulgence in the future." Company commanders had complete discretion over who received passes and usually based their judgement on prior behavior. As a result, Lieutenant George Davis refused to issue a twenty-four hour pass to Private Charles Smith a month after he had been arrested in Mackinaw City for being absent without leave in March 1889. Smith who had four previous garrison court martial convictions in less than four months, went to St. Ignace anyway and was arrested when he returned to the fort the next day. For his night on the town Smith was sentenced to six months in the fort prison cell before being dishonorably discharged from the army.[136]

Fort Mackinac soldiers occasionally enjoyed a welcome break from the monotony of their daily routine. Prior to 1889, Sunday duty was limited but included the weekly inspection. Typical was the schedule of Sunday, November 30, 1879 when first call for inspection was sounded at 8:50 a.m. The men assembled with their rifles on the parade ground (or in their quarters in winter) ten minutes later where company commanders performed a thorough inspection of dress, grooming and weapons. After the inspection, officers toured the guardhouse, barracks, hospital and other buildings paying careful attention to the cleanliness and care given each facility. Soldiers enjoyed additional free time beginning in June 1889 when the army moved weekly inspections to Saturdays and the soldiers were given a full day off on Sunday except for guard and police duty.[137]

Holidays were always popular with soldiers who appreciated the opportunity for recreation and relaxation. Thanksgiving, Christmas, New Year's Day, Washington's Birthday, Decoration Day and the Fourth of July were the holidays most often recognized by company commanders. Usually all duties were suspended on these days except for guard mounting, policing and roll calls. Soldiers used their free time to rest in the barracks, play cards, visit the village, or travel to nearby towns.

The United States army had a special affinity for the Fourth of July. Fort Mackinac soldiers usually celebrated the holiday with a variety of ceremonial and recreational activities. A hand-picked squad fired the national salute – one round for each state of the Union – from the fort cannons at daybreak. In 1873 Captain Leslie Smith dispensed with the firing "in consequence of a serious illness of a prominent citizen…" but took the opportunity to have the Declaration of Independence read to his men.[138] Soldiers spent the rest of the day playing games, relaxing in the park or joining civilians in village-sponsored activities. In 1886 soldiers ran in foot races, squared off against Cheboygan in a rifle match, played baseball against the St. Ignace club and enjoyed a special dinner with deserts of peach and raspberry pie, cherries, strawberries and cream and ginger snaps. A reporter for the *Cheboygan Democrat* proudly reported that "Very little drunkenness was seen on the street, something very uncommon for the 4th of July."[139]

Chapter V

Discipline and Punishment

DISCIPLINE WAS ESSENTIAL to the smooth operation of Fort Mackinac. With a garrison of up to eighty soldiers involved in many complex tasks it was necessary for officers to maintain strict military order, a respect for authority and adherence to rules and regulations. To ensure discipline the army established a code of military justice known as the Articles of War. This congressionally-approved document articulated military crimes and provided a system of courts to deal with violators. Both garrison and general courts marital were used to try Fort Mackinac soldiers accused of military crimes during the period 1867-1895. Military trials were very time consuming and officers frequently complained about the hundreds of hours they devoted to court martial duty every year. The problem was not just a matter of discipline, but also a cumbersome judicial system that did not provide efficient and timely disciplinary action. Summary courts, adopted in 1890, helped streamline the process of military justice.

Garrison courts were convened to deal with minor crimes such as insubordination, absence without leave and dereliction of duty. The courts were convened by the post commander and consisted of four officers, three serving as court members and one acting as judge advocate. The judge advocate guided the legal proceedings of each case. He read the charges, administered the oaths, arraigned prisoners and questioned witnesses. He had the challenging task of prosecuting the case for the government while providing legal advice to the prisoner for his defense. Garrison courts could impose maximum penalties of one month incarceration in the guardhouse and loss of one month's pay. While non-commissioned officers were usually spared jail time and cash fines, they almost always lost the pay and benefits of their rank as they were reduced to privates. With no other means of discipline at their disposal, officers used

An accused soldier pleads his case in the 1880's court martial reenactment on the fort parade ground.

garrison courts martial to deal with nearly every minor breech of conduct at Fort Mackinac. Between 1884 and 1890 alone, Fort Mackinac officers tried 309 garrison courts martial cases involving hundreds of hours of work managing prisoners, acquiring evidence and conducting trials.

General courts martial, authorized by the division commander at the request of the post commandant, dealt with more serious crimes such as desertion, thievery and assault and battery. These courts also were used to try commissioned officers accused of military crimes. General courts required a minimum of six officers, five serving on the court and a sixth who was judge advocate. There were only seventy-two general courts martial cases tried at Fort Mackinac between 1868 and 1890 and a soldier facing one of these tribunals knew that he was in deep trouble. Sentences for soldiers convicted in general courts could include dishonorable discharge, long term confinement in a military penitentiary and severe cash fines. Corporal punishment, including flogging and branding, was outlawed before the Civil War. For a short period after the war, convicted soldiers were sometimes punished by having to carry extra weight all day. Privates Joseph Johnson and Fredrick Lane were both found guilty of being drunk on duty by a general court martial on July 24, 1872. Their punishment included carrying a loaded knapsack weighing 24 pounds all day from reveille to retreat.[140] By the mid-1870s such "cruel punishments" were no longer administered in military courts.

Captain Joseph Bush was the only commissioned officer to face a general court martial at Fort Mackinac after the Civil War. Regimental commander Colonel David Stanley traveled from Detroit to preside over the trial which included an eight-man court with Lieutenant James Chester of the 3rd Artillery serving as judge advocate. Bush, who pled not guilty, was arrested and confined to his quarters for being drunk on duty on three separate occasions in May and June 1876. After the prosecution presented its case, Bush rebutted each specification with a long list of witnesses (both soldiers and civilians) who testified to the captain's sobriety. Bush's attorney, James J. Brown, concluded the defense by reading a fifty-page summary detailing his client's innocence. The court was swayed by the argument that what appeared as drunkenness was nothing more than "a naturally excitable and nervous temperament," and acquitted the captain on the charge and all specifications.[141]

Dr. Charles Woodruff, Fort Mackinac post surgeon 1887-1889.

Captain Bush was but one of a long list of Fort Mackinac soldiers accused of alcohol abuse, the major cause of military discipline problems. Soldiers were court martialed for being drunk at nearly every conceivable military activity including drill, guard, kitchen police, roll call, fatigue and while on duty as nurses in the post hospital. They were found drunk in their quarters, in the guardhouse, in the kitchen, on the parade ground and in the village. Drunken soldiers got in fights, went AWOL, stole money, broke into private homes, disobeyed orders and neglected duty. Although alcohol abuse knew no season, there was a particularly high incidence of trouble following pay day and at the end of the summer. September was typically a busy month in the Fort Mackinac judicial system. Dr. Charles Woodruff explained the September 1887 "epidemic of drunkenness and general deviltry" as a result of "the departure of numerous female employees of the various summer hotels just closed, each departure being mourned by a 'drunk.'" The post surgeon went on to comment:

> It is to be regretted that no check can be placed on the rum-sellers of the Island who blew the men of their little money and fill them with whiskey. In theory the soldier is to blame, but as forbidden fruit is always sweetest, it is taken in excess when the chance occurs. The temptation being lessened the drunkenness would decline[142]

Most alcohol-related crimes were dealt with by garrison courts martial but repeated misconduct would sometimes result in more serious charges. Private John Lyons was tried and convicted by a garrison court marital of being drunk on duty three times in September and October 1883. For the first offense he was fined five dollars, the second time he lost another five dollars and spent five days confined at hard labor and for the third offense Lyons was confined at hard labor for thirty days. These punishments had little effect on Lyons' behavior and he was arrested again on November 8, 1883 for being "so drunk as to be unable to perform any military duty." This time a general court martial ended his military career when it convicted him of multiple violations of the 62nd Article of War – conduct "to the prejudice of good order and military discipline." Lyons was dishonorably discharged and sent to Fort Leavenworth military prison for a year.[143]

Following a similar path of self destruction, Private Henry Coon was arrested for being drunk at tattoo roll call on January 3, 1889 just two weeks after he arrived at Fort Mackinac. Coon was convicted by a garrison court and given a rather light fine of two dollars and fifty cents. The Ohio-born private was tried twice more by garrison courts before his misconduct landed him in front of a general court martial in May 1889. Accused of being drunk while on duty as chief cook, Coon compounded his problems by resisting arrest and calling five-foot, four-inch tall sergeant George Robinson a "damned little cur." Not surprisingly, Coon was convicted and fined thirty dollars and imprisoned at hard labor for three months. While in the Fort Mackinac jail cell during the summer of 1889 Coon carved his initials "H.L.C." in the prison window sill.[144]

Married soldiers, especially those with children, faced added pressures that sometimes led to discipline problems. Although the army refused to enlist married men, there was no prohibition against them getting married once they joined the service. After privates Oliver and Hillengahs married hotel servants and deserted in 1887, a frustrated Captain Goodale complained that company commanders should be given the authority to forbid their men from marrying without permission "under penalty of trial for disobedience of orders."[145] Not all soldiers deserted to follow their wives, some fled the fort to escape a souring relationship. In 1877 Commissary Sergeant Edward Raymond deserted after eight years of faithful service at Fort Mackinac. Major Alfred Hough listed his unhappy marriage as one of the reasons that this once "excellent soldier" fled the army. Six years later Private Charles Mahar married island resident Julia O'Mara in August 1883 and their daughter Rosetta was born one month later. Apparently the pressure of an instant family became too much for Mahar to bear and he deserted because of "domestic troubles" on October 16, 1883.[146]

Occasionally, marital infidelity pitted two soldiers against each other with potentially murderous results. In June 1873 post blacksmith Private William Bowman separated from his wife Elizabeth because of a relationship she developed with Corporal Frank Burrell. Two weeks after reconciling with his wife, Bowman caught Burrell in his house with his wife and made a formal complaint to the post commander without getting any satisfaction. When Bowman found Burrell and his wife walking home from a play at the McLeod House in the village that evening, the irate blacksmith vowed revenge. In a fit of rage, Bowman grabbed a rifle from the gun rack in the company quarters, loaded the weapon and confronted Burrell promising to put a bullet through him if he didn't stay away from his wife. Bowman was immediately arrested and hauled before a general court martial two weeks later where he pled guilty. In a letter to the court the repentant private tried to explain the emotions that led him to such a desperate act: "thinking of my wife's perfidy, my mind became diseased at the time, brooding over my happiness thus blasted and hopes of life fled forever." Bowman implored the officers to consider his prior good behavior and give him clemency. The court, moved by his plea, found Bowman guilty but immediately released him with nothing more than a reprimand from post commandant Leslie Smith.[147]

Desertion was a recurring problem and a major concern for the United States army in the late nineteenth century. Described by General Nelson Miles as "the principle evil besetting the army," desertion accounted for 88,475 soldiers leaving the ranks between 1868 and 1891.[148] Throughout the period 1867 to 1895 thirteen percent of the soldiers at Fort Mackinac deserted, slightly lower than the national average. The greatest flood of desertions occurred between 1869 and 1874 when 25 percent of Captain Leslie Smith's company left the fort. Many of these soldiers bolted as a result of Congress' decision to reduce the army pay scale to pre-Civil War levels. Consistent with the national trend, most soldiers (77 percent) deserted Fort Mackinac within the first eighteen months after they enlisted. Like Private William Houck, who joined the army in February 1878, arrived at Fort Mackinac in April and deserted three weeks later on May 14, these soldiers were in long enough to become disillusioned with military life but not long enough to enjoy any of the benefits of longevity.[149] May was a popular month for Fort Mackinac deserters who had waited until the end of winter for their chance to escape military life. The desertion rate remained high during the summers, peaking in July when the warm weather and increased boat traffic provided the best opportunity to leave.

Most Fort Mackinac deserters were never apprehended, but those captured usually faced a general court martial and severe punishment. During the night of April 5, 1873 privates George Cain and Thomas Mullin snuck out of Fort Mackinac just before tattoo roll call. The fleeing soldiers arranged for Antoine Vassar to meet them with his horse and cutter on the frozen bay in town. Vassar, with his sleigh partially hidden on one end of the town dock, met the soldiers as arranged and took them to his house on the mainland near Cheboygan. When Cain and Mullen failed to show up for roll call Captain Smith, acting upon a tip from a local resident, ordered Lieutenant Thomas Sharpe and Corporal Theodore Weaver to follow and apprehend the deserters. Sharpe and Weaver crossed the ice and arrived at Vassar's house the next morning where they found the fleeing culprits hiding under a bed. The men were returned to Fort Mackinac and thrown in the prison cell until a general court martial was convened three months later. Both men were convicted of desertion and sentenced to be

The Straits of Mackinac from Fort Mackinac's southwest sentry box.

©1993 THOMAS KACHADURIAN

dishonorably discharged and sent to a military prison for two years. While Mullin was discharged and incarcerated at Fort Wayne the jury requested clemency for Cain, citing his prior faithful service and "good conduct since his arrest, indicating repentance." The reviewing officers approved the recommendation and sentenced Cain to nine months in the Fort Mackinac cell and a fine of ten dollars a month for an equal period of time. Upon release, Cain rejoined his company.[150]

Army officials, embarrassed and concerned about the high rate of desertion, began a systematic study of the problem in 1882. In order to discover the underlying causes for desertion, the army directed post commanders to submit annual reports listing each soldier who deserted. Further, commanders were expected to give a reason for each soldier's departure. On August 12, 1884 Captain George Brady sent a list of seventeen soldiers who had deserted Fort Mackinac during the past year. According to Brady, three left because of "general dissatisfaction" with the army and another three deserted as a result of "women's influence" including private Gilbert Jamison who "eloped with a married woman." Private C. S. Paquette was listed as a "malingerer" who intentionally shot off his right fore finger about a year before he deserted. Brady ascribed "drunkenness" as the motivation for seven deserters while "no cause" could be found for two of the missing soldiers.[151] Commandants' reports in subsequent years listed many of the same motivations along with gambling debts as the primary causes for desertion.

While Captain Brady argued that longer prison sentences would discourage desertion, others insisted that improving the quality of military life would be more effective. To this end, military reform measures of the 1880s were designed to reduce desertion by improving soldiers' clothing, housing, diet and sanitation and encouraging recreational opportunities including sports activities and post canteens. In 1886 Captain Goodale was thrilled to report that only two men had deserted in the last year and he attributed his success to fresh vegetables from the garden, a modern new bathhouse, the post reading room with a billiard table and the easy duty. "The men," Goodale reported, "generally are more contented than at any post I have ever seen."[152]

George K. Brady, Fort Mackinac commander 1884-1886.

PENNSYLVANIA HISTORICAL AND MUSEUM COMMISSION

Military reforms in the 1890s continued to improve the soldier's lot while decreasing the desertion rate. Most importantly, the army realized the need to provide some legal way for soldiers to leave the service before their term expired. As early as 1887 Colonel Richard Dodge argued that the "contract of enlistment" was "too rigid, too binding." While providing no specific plan, Dodge argued that, "To hold a man for five years…is too much like slavery to meet the requirements of the charitable enlightenment of our age and country."[153] Congress resolved the problem in 1890 when "An Act to Prevent Desertion and for Other Purposes" allowed a soldier to purchase his discharge after one year of service. After three years in the army a soldier could take a three-month furlough and even leave the service without paying a penalty.[154] Many Fort Mackinac soldiers jumped at the chance to take a vacation. Private Noah Blankenship went on furlough in March 1891 and enjoyed civilian life so much that he filed for and received his honorable discharge and never returned to the island. Austrian-born Corporal James Duda began his three-month furlough on February 1, 1893 – three years to the day after he enlisted. Unlike Blankenship, however, Duda returned to the army and was soon promoted to sergeant.[155] As a result of this act and other military reforms, the army's desertion rate plummeted to a rate of about five percent in the 1890s. The results were even more dramatic at Fort Mackinac where only three percent of the soldiers deserted between 1890 and 1895.[156]

Congress passed two bills in 1890 that provided much needed reform to the army's judicial system. The first act required military courts to provide every soldier facing a

MARQUETTE COUNTY HISTORICAL SOCIETY

Lieutenant Benjamin C. Morse and friend enjoy a panoramic view from the West Bluff, ca. 1890.

general court martial with a suitable officer to serve as legal counsel. This policy addressed the impossible situation of having the judge advocate serve as both prosecutor for the army and advisor to prisoners. The second bill created an entirely new judicial process called summary courts.

Designed to prosecute soldiers accused of minor offenses, summary courts consisted of a single officer who was second in command of the post and stipulated that the trial was to take place within twenty-four hours of the soldier's arrest. Like garrison courts, soldiers found guilty by these tribunals could be imprisoned at hard labor for no more than one month and fined a maximum of one month's pay. These courts were not only more efficient for post administrators, they also addressed the problem of soldiers being incarcerated for long periods awaiting trial. Soldiers arrested in the early 1870s spent as long as a week in the post guardhouse before trial. By contrast Private William Sullivan, accused of being absent without leave, was arraigned, tried, found guilty, fined two dollars and released by a summary court – all on the same day in 1893. Under the provisions of the law, accused soldiers could still request a garrison court martial. Hoping to find some support in a larger venue, privates James McManus and Henry Phillips both pleaded not guilty in one of the few garrison courts that met in 1891. The strategy paid off for Phillips who was acquitted of being "noisy and boisterous in the streets of Mackinac." McManus, facing the same charge as Phillips with the additional indictment of evading arrest and running away, was found guilty and fined five dollars.[157] The introduction of summary courts and other improvements in the army's judicial process were generally hailed as positive reforms and well received by officers and enlisted men alike.

Chapter VI

Non – Military Garrison Life

FORT MACKINAC WAS A COMMUNITY OF MEN, women and children who had interests and obligations beyond the daily grind of military life. For married soldiers, off-duty activities usually centered around wives and children. Many soldiers used their free time for recreation and sports while others pursued hobbies, social interests or spiritual growth. These diverse activities offered soldiers relief from the monotony of repetitive army tasks and made the garrison a much more interesting place to live.

Women and children were an important part of the fort community between 1867 and 1895. The majority of Fort Mackinac officers were married and most had children. Significantly fewer enlisted men were married because of the army's prohibition against accepting married soldiers. Nevertheless, more than forty enlisted men married after arriving at Fort Mackinac and several more transferred to the island with their wives.

Unmarried soldiers with an eye towards romance and matrimony had ample opportunities for finding companionship among the island's permanent population. If he could not find his true love among the locals, a soldier could wait until summer when the influx of seasonal employees brought dozens of maids, servants, cooks, sales clerks and nurses to the island. Marriage was particularly popular at the fort in 1878 when ten enlisted men and two officers were married. Thirty-three year old Private William Dion exchanged vows with Jane, daughter of island shoemaker Antoine Mirandette. Like Mirandette, Dion was French Canadian. Annie McGulpin, daughter of island laborer Benjamin McGulpin, married Irish-born Private Patrick Tobin on May 19, 1878. Marriage had no ill effect on Tobin's military career as he was promoted twice within six months of his wedding. Three years later Annie's sister Elizabeth also found true love at Fort Mackinac when she married Private Charles Wehner. Like many

Mackinac Island's scenic roads and trails provided soldiers with the perfect environment for summer romance.

local girls who married soldiers, Annie was able to convince her husband to move to Mackinac Island after he left the service. The Wehners enjoyed more than fifty years of marriage before Elizabeth passed away in 1933. Charles died twenty years later and was buried next to his beloved wife in the island's Roman Catholic cemetery.[158]

Single officers garnered considerable attention from Mackinac's unmarried female population, especially those from the upper crust of island society. In December 1878 Lieutenant John McAdam Webster married Rose Van Allen whose father owned the Island House Hotel. One month later her friend Rosa Truscott, a twenty-five-year-old widow and daughter of general store owner George Truscott, walked down the aisle with Captain Charles Webb. After Webster retired from the army, he returned to Mackinac and helped Rose run the Island House. Rosa Webb also returned, but without her husband who died of pneumonia at Fort McKavett just two years after they were married. Stung by the loss of two husbands, Rosa devoted the rest of her life to Mackinac Island cultural and civic activities. She founded Michigan's first Girl Scout troop on the island in 1921 and helped organize a Boy Scout troop as well. She established the island's first library, served on the hospital board of trustees, was an active member of Trinity Episcopal Church and helped preserve the historic Stuart House.[159]

Army wives kept busy caring for children, buying food and managing domestic chores while their husbands were engaged in military duties. Most were happy to be at Fort Mackinac, especially if they transferred from a more isolated and less comfortable frontier post. Compared to Fort Craig on the desolate plains of New Mexico with no grass, no school and no playmates for the children, Fort Mackinac was an oasis for Mary Cowles and her family. Her island home was spacious, well maintained and perched high on the island's southern bluff with a panoramic view over the Straits of Mackinac. Transferring to Fort Mackinac was a homecoming for Lieutenant Edward Pratt who grew up in the island fort when his father was post commandant in the late 1850s. Pratt returned to his childhood home in the officers' stone quarters which had also been occupied by his grandfather, Captain John Clitz, who commanded the fort in the 1830s. Every officer enjoyed at least three bedrooms, a large parlor, dining room, well-equipped kitchen and living space for servants.

The officers' stone quarters parlor of Lieutenant Benjamin C. Morse and Jessie Cable Morse soon after they were married in 1890.

Benjamin C. Morse and Jessie Cable Morse.

Nearly every officer, and a few married enlisted men who could afford the expense, had servants to assist with the time-consuming job of caring for children and maintaining a late nineteenth-century household. Seven servants lived at Fort Mackinac in 1880 including the young Irish-born sisters Mary and Margaret Costilo. Fifteen-year old Mary lived with Captain Charles and Marguerite Davis and her sister worked as a servant at the post hospital. Even Private Patrick McNamara and his wife Jane had a servant, Eliza, who helped care for their three young boys.[160]

Although the married enlisted men's quarters were not as spacious or well situated with lake views as the officers' residences, they were comfortable and well equipped. Occasionally the number of married men exceeded the available quarters and, as a result, enlisted men's wives were sometimes forced to find housing in the village. With permission from the commandant, a soldier could live in town with his wife. This type of arrangement, however, was frowned upon by most officers who had a difficult time regulating the activities of soldiers living outside the garrison. In June 1891 Major Edwin Coates rejected Private Plosier's request to transfer to the island post from Fort Wayne, Detroit. Coates had no room for Ploiser and his wife in the fort and complained that he already had seven married enlisted men living in the village.[161]

Enlisted men's wives could supplement their husbands' wages by working as a servant for an officer or as a company laundress or hospital matron. Helen Temple, wife of First Sergeant Robert Temple, worked as a domestic servant for Captain and Mrs. Joseph Bush. Before moving to Fort Mackinac both Robert and Helen lived with the Bushes in officers' quarters. At Mackinac, however, Captain Bush deemed his quarters too small and let the Temples occupy them while he took up residence in the town.[162]

Sergeant James Martin and Helen Delaney were married in 1888 while Martin was stationed at Fort Mackinac.

The army had a tradition stretching back to the eighteenth century of having women, usually wives of non-commissioned officers, wash soldiers' clothes. Each company was allowed to employ up to four laundresses who received food, housing, fuel and the services of the post surgeon. Laundresses lived with their families in the dilapidated officers' wood quarters on the south side of the parade ground until a new six-unit residence was constructed behind the fort in 1878. A council of administration consisting of two or three officers set the monthly price for laundry service at one dollar per soldier in 1872. The lone laundress who worked in the fort that year brought home about thirty dollars a month, a nice supplement to her husband's army salary. Laundresses were appointed by company commanders who insisted that they follow garrison rules and regulations. They were required to maintain their quarters, be present at the weekly inspections and behave in a responsible and respectable manner. Captain Leslie Smith fired laundress Mrs. Lewis Perry in February 1870 "in consequence of drunkenness and disgraceful conduct while at a theatrical performance in the town of Mackinac." Mrs. Perry, whose husband had died just three months earlier, not only lost her job but was also immediately evicted from her quarters.[163]

In a cost-cutting move the army banned the use of government-supported laundresses in 1878. Women serving in this capacity were allowed to continue to receive army rations and housing until the end of their husband's enlistment. While army wives no longer received military benefits beginning in the mid-1880s, many continued to live in Fort Mackinac housing and bring in extra money doing the soldiers' laundry.

Enlisted men's wives also worked as matrons at the post hospital. There was usually a single matron, "generally the wife of some well-behaved and good soldier," who was responsible for housekeeping and laundry. More than a dozen women, almost always the wives of non-commissioned officers or hospital stewards, worked at the fort

Captain Greenleaf Goodale, standing, with his father George and two sons, George and Roy, ca. 1885.

hospital between 1872 and 1892. Nettie Pauly earned ten dollars a month as hospital matron while working alongside her husband, Hospital Steward Louis Pauly, in the early 1880s.[164]

Many married couples living at Fort Mackinac were blessed with children who became an important part of the garrison community and social structure. Calvin and Mary Cowles had a large family even by nineteenth-century standards. Mary bore seven children at seven different posts between 1875 and 1887. She was pregnant more than forty percent of the time during this twelve and one-half year period. Josiah was only four months old when the Cowles made the 2,000 mile move from Fort Craig, New Mexico to Fort Mackinac in 1884. When the family returned to the island in 1887 after two years in New York, Mary not only had to organize her four small children including the baby David, but she was also six months pregnant with Isabel. Mary's pregnancies were not particularly difficult despite the size of her babies. Two of the newborn "busters" weighed eleven pounds including Isabel, "a fun, healthy baby" delivered by Post Surgeon Dr. Charles Woodruff on November 5, 1887. The Cowles did not plan on having such a large family. In fact, after the birth of their third child in 1878 Calvin confidently announced that he and Mary were "willing to rest on our laurels…and stop recruiting." The enlistments continued, however, and they added four more recruits.[165]

Parents spent a good deal of time caring for their children, especially the young ones. Even with the help of a servant, a soldier's wife spent most of her day feeding, bathing, nursing, disciplining and playing with her children. Younger children often played in and around the family home. During the restoration of the officers' stone quarters in the early 1970s carpenters found marbles, spinning tops, playing cards and toy soldiers left behind or lost by children who once lived there. Nine-year-old Toosie Cowles played with a chatterbox that she received from her grandparents and Mary Louise Pratt enjoyed her "wonderball." Given to her when she was sick and confined to quarters, this delightful toy was a large ball of yarn filled with little toys and treasures to be discovered as Mary slowly unwrapped the threads.[166]

The joy of parenthood was occasionally replaced by the heartbreak of a child's untimely death. High infant mortality rates, a sad reality of nineteenth-century

Fort Mackinac's stone quarters provided two apartments for officers and their families.

American life, claimed many victims at Fort Mackinac. Rosetta Mahar, whose father deserted Fort Mackinac in October 1883, died just fifteen months later when she was only a year and a half old. Four years later young Lena Baseler lay dying at her home in the village below the fort while her father was in the post jail serving a three-month sentence for being absent without leave. Captain Goodale sought and received approval from the division commander to release Baseler long enough to visit his sick child. Lena died two days later and was buried in the post cemetery

Nor were the offspring of commissioned officers spared fatal illnesses. Calvin and Mary Cowles lost three of their seven children to childhood diseases, two while stationed at Fort Mackinac. Josiah did not fare well after the long trip from New Mexico and Calvin reported that he was "a little sick" in July 1884 while expressing hope he would "be well in a day or so." Though his son's condition worsened, Calvin remained optimistic, promising to send his father a photograph of the baby in August. Less than a month later Josiah died of an intestinal infection in the family quarters. Calvin expressed his profound sorrow in a letter to his father the next day:

> Our dear little baby died of bowel troubles at about one o'clock yesterday morning, after a brief but painful illness. His poor, tired little body now sleeps neath the shade in the beautiful cemetery at this post. We are overwhelmed and crushed by the terrible and sudden affliction but feel that everything was done for him that the doctor's skill or our love could suggest, and we humbly bow our heads in submission to the will of Him who doth all things well.

Four years later Isabel Cowles died at Fort Mackinac just a few weeks after her first birthday. Following a funeral service in Trinity Episcopal Church, Calvin and Mary buried their young daughter next to Josiah at the post cemetery.[167]

As children grew their playground expanded into the fort and to the larger island community. Harold Corbusier, son of post surgeon Dr. William Corbusier, and his brothers explored the old fort and made a collection of military buttons and other artifacts. They played in island caves, made syrup from maple trees, had picnics on Round Island, skated on the frozen bay and went sledding in the winter. Holiday celebrations provided memorable experiences for the Corbusier children They exchanged Easter cards at Sunday School, watched fireworks on the Fourth of July, exchanged presents at Christmas and bobbed for potatoes (apples weren't available) on All Hallow's Eve.[168] Like the Corbusier boys, most children enjoyed their time on Mackinac Island and found it a delightful and fascinating place to play. Their recreation, however, was not always appreciated by post commanders who admonished parents to keep a close watch over the behavior of their children.

Not surprisingly, children roaming free around the fort sometimes got in trouble. Exasperated by the conduct of children playing in the lumber piles near the coal house, Captain Sellers posted a general order in September 1879 warning parents that they would be held responsible for any further vandalism. Fights between older boys occa-

Dr. William and Fanny Corbusier with their sons (left to right) Francis, Harold, William, Philip and Claude in 1893.

CORBUSIER COLLECTION

sionally disrupted garrison peace. Jerry Ryan, son of Corporal William and Joanna Ryan, was known as a tough kid, often picking fights with village children. Ryan, however, met his match when he fought to a draw with Claude Corbusier outside the officers' hill quarters in the early 1880s.[169]

One way parents kept children out of trouble was by putting them in school. Fort Mackinac children usually received their education in the village school except for a few years in the 1880s when they attended classes at the post school house. Trustees of the island's Union School, located in the old Indian Dormitory, opened their doors to fort children soon after soldiers returned to Fort Mackinac following the Civil War. Captain Mitchell was so pleased with their generosity that he requested permission to give the trustees his allotment of "fuel allowed for schools and library purposes." After the post schoolhouse was built in 1879, soldiers' children received their education in the fort when suitable teachers were available and a sufficient number of students were present. John Devlin, a forty-three year old Irish-born corporal, was the school's first teacher. In 1882 he was replaced by Sergeant Frederick J. Grant who held classes five and a half hours a day, September through May. Grant delighted in telling the children about his days as a student and all about the mischievous tricks he played on his teachers. When the boys pulled these same pranks on Grant, the indignant teacher marched them down to the commandant for discipline. One of their favorite times of the day was drill exercise when Grant would treat them like soldiers, barking out his commands in strict disciplinarian style. Grant was replaced by Private Crawford Anderson who was probably less fun than the colorful sergeant but made sure the children got an education. He taught them spelling, reading, geography, history, arithmetic and writing. In 1883 Anderson had a total of nine students, including the children of Captain Sellers, Dr. Corbusier and Private William Ryan.[170]

Children of the post returned to village classrooms in the mid-1880s until Private

FORT VERDE STATE HISTORIC PARK

Mary Hitchcock Cowles and Calvin
Cowles, Jr.

Benedict Landau reopened the post
school in the fall of 1887. Landau, a thir-
ty-five-year old native of Constantinople,
Turkey, was a trained school teacher.
Earning an extra fifty-cents a day as post school teacher, Landau developed a cur-
riculum, purchased schoolbooks and supplies and prepared the schoolhouse for its
young students. Landau's class included Toosie, Willie and Calvin Cowles who had
just returned with their family after nearly three years in New York. When the Cowles
family and the rest of the Twenty-third Infantry left in 1890, the fort children once
again attended the town school where they remained until the fort closed five years
later.[171]

Service at Fort Mackinac provided officers and enlisted men with liberal amounts
of free time and many opportunities to pursue recreational and social activities. Soldiers
enjoyed many sporting activities but none more than baseball. Americans from urban
parks to rural playgrounds became enamored with baseball as they tried to forget the
devastation of the Civil War in the late 1860s. Baseball's popularity soon spread to
Mackinac and as early as 1871 Fort Mackinac soldiers regularly played baseball with
the encouragement of the post commandant. By the mid-1880s baseball was all the
rage and even the officers caught the fever and took an increasing role in supporting
the fort team. Lieutenant Edward Pratt helped form the Fort Mackinac Base Ball Club
in 1885. The thirty-two-year old lieutenant became the team captain and contributed

the first four dollars to the club fund that paid for two new bats at forty-cents each and a "League" baseball which cost one-dollar and twenty-five cents. By mid-summer the team had several bats and balls, three bases, a catcher's mask and a carefully laid out diamond on the large parade ground behind the fort. With a copy of Spaulding's *Base Ball Guide* in hand, Pratt and his men took the field.[172]

The highlight of the 1885 season was a two-game series with the highly-touted Diamond Baseball Club of Cheboygan. The first game was played in Cheboygan as a part of the city's Fourth of July celebration. Most of the fort officers and enlisted men accompanied the team and cheered for the Fort Nine. The fort's starting lineup featured the strong-armed blacksmith Private Hiram Eddy on the mound with First Sergeant Thomas Hennessey behind the plate. Corporal William Sconce, one of the regiment's finest sharpshooters, patrolled left field while club treasurer Corporal Charles Hastings played shortstop. In a move sure to curry favor with the commandant, the team chose Captain Brady's seventeen-year-old son Mifflin to play right field. Fireworks came early to Cheboygan that day as the bats for both teams exploded. When the dust cleared, the soldiers were victorious, outslugging their opponents seventeen to ten.[173]

Flush with success and the twenty-five dollar prize money, the soldiers invested in new uniforms. They bought eighteen yards of flannel and paid nearly twenty dollars for tailored suits complete with elastic fittings. The soldiers proudly wore their new uniforms when the Diamonds traveled to Mackinac Island on August 14 for the rematch. The Cheboygan team came well prepared to avenge their earlier loss and defeated the soldiers. In his journal Dr. Bailey remarked that the Cheboygan team had little reason to brag, however, since they "smuggled in three professional players from abroad."[174]

The soldiers' baseball field was laid out on the parade ground behind Fort Mackinac. Soldiers built the grandstand to the far left in 1887.

Soldiers on the Fort Mackinac dock posing with the garrison sailboat, ca. 1887.

The fort baseball team continued to flourish while the Twenty-third Infantry was stationed at Mackinac. Corporal Robert "Tug" Wilson became the team's official scorer and scheduled games with teams from cities around northern Michigan including Mackinaw City, Sault Ste. Marie, Harbor Springs, Petoskey and Reed City. Wilson, who served as a part-time reporter for the *Cheboygan Democrat*, submitted box scores and game summaries to the paper which chronicled the team's progress throughout the summer months in the late 1880s. Fort officers continued to support the team and even allowed the men to construct a grandstand capable of seating 500 spectators. The soldiers charged a twenty-five cent admission to their home games, with seating in the grandstand costing ten cents extra.[175]

Although baseball was most popular, soldiers enjoyed other recreational activities. Sportsmen hunted whitetail deer and grouse on the nearby islands and fished for brook trout, walleye and perch in Straits area streams and lakes. Captain William Manning, an avid angler, took his family fishing near Petoskey in July 1886 and journeyed with friends to the Les Cheneaux Islands for perch fishing a few weeks later.[176] Sharpshooting officers and enlisted men combined forces on the fort's rifle team which, like the baseball club, competed against other northern Michigan squads. Enlisted men on pass used the post sailboat for short excursions to nearby towns or a cruise around the island. In 1875 Major Hough gave orders that the boat could be used only with a non-commissioned officer present and that no intoxicating liquors be taken aboard.[177] Whether or not alcohol was involved, three soldiers using the boat in 1891 nearly lost their lives.

The soldiers set sail from the island at about 11:00 on the morning of November

23, 1891 bound for St. Ignace, a distance of about five miles. While moderate winds prevailed in the island's sheltered harbor, the soldiers encountered a brisk "half gale" and heavy seas in the open water. Crashing waves sent an unremitting spray of water over the gunwales and about half way across the Straits the company boat capsized, leaving the three frightened soldiers clinging to the floating wreck in the chilly November water. Carpenters working on the south side of the island witnessed the accident and alerted Frank Lasley and Nicholas Shomin who took quick action. The two men broke down the door of a nearby shed where a rowboat was stored for the winter. With the help of several friends, they lowered the boat on ropes down the "precipitous side" of a one-hundred-and-fifty-foot bluff to the lake shore. Lasley and Shomin, at considerable risk to their own lives, launched the small vessel and set off for the imperiled men. With great effort, they reached the capsized boat and dragged the waterlogged and half-frozen men from the lake beginning with forty-three year old Sergeant Richard Shute, who was the most exhausted. All five men returned safely to the island and the soldiers quickly recovered. A year later both Shomin and Lasley received a gold life-saving medal of honor from Charles Foster, Secretary of the United States Treasury Department, the agency that operated the United States Life Saving Service.[178]

The onslaught of cold weather did not curtail recreational activities as soldiers found many ways to enjoy Mackinac's snow and ice in the winter. Favorite pastimes included ice skating and sledding. Dr. Corbusier and sons Claude and Harold skated

Ice boats skim across Mackinac Island's frozen bay.

The officers' stone quarters parlor of Lieutenant Edward and Kate Pratt, ca. 1888. Kate's piano occupied a prominent place in the room and provided music for a variety of festive occasions.

on the ice in front of the fort in the 1880s. The inventive doctor even built bamboo pole sails that they used to carry them along the ice. Fanny Corbusier joined her husband and sons but declined to skate, preferring rather to be pushed along in a sled. Others enjoyed the thrill of sailing across the frozen bay in sleek ice boats. Lieutenant George Davis took Captain Manning's niece for a harrowing ride on February 4, 1889. The boat hit thin ice and plummeted both crew and riders into the frigid waters. Although he escaped drowning, Davis was deeply embarrassed when he returned his drenched date to her uncle.[179]

Coasting down the snow-covered hill just west of the fort was an equally popular and dangerous winter sport. The entire garrison, from young children to senior officers, enjoyed sledding on Fort Hill. Using toboggans, sleds and sleighs they flew down the hill and coasted to a gentle stop on the bay. Mrs. Sellers and Mrs. Plummer, unfamiliar with the normal landing area, miscalculated and plunged their sled into a water hole that villagers kept open for drinking water. Though safe, their clothes were frozen stiff before they reached a nearby house. Open water was not the only danger, sometimes the ride itself was treacherous. During one sledding party fort soldiers decided to try running an old row boat down the hill and the unfortunate steersman ended up with a broken leg.[180]

Fort Mackinac soldiers also enjoyed a wide variety of social activities in their free time. Most social interaction consisted of informal gatherings in the fort. Enlisted men enjoyed card games and could often be found in the early evening gathered around the squad room tables playing poker, cribbage or whist. Others played billiards or board games in the canteen, learned new tunes on their musical instruments or read the

MARQUETTE COUNTY HISTORICAL SOCIETY

Market Street with Fort Mackinac in the distance and the John Jacob Astor House to the left.

latest newspapers or magazines in the reading room. An officers' quarters was the scene of many informal gatherings from dinner parties to holiday celebrations. Often the event was accompanied by music as several officers' wives were accomplished musicians including Mary Cowles who played melodeon and Anna Bush who played guitar. Kate Pratt's piano had a prominent location in her stone quarters parlor and she played for many festive family gatherings.

In the fall of 1887 enlisted men from Companies E and K, Twenty-third Infantry formed the Fort Mackinac Social Club to provide activities for the "long winter months." Fort officers supported the club and gave them use of a large, well furnished room which included a piano leased from the Astor House. While most evenings were spent singing and dancing around the piano, the club room was also the scene for more formal occasions such as a farewell reception for First Sergeant Charles Hastings in February 1888. The departing sergeant was completely surprised when he entered the club room and found it decorated with evergreens, flags and a large photo of himself with the word "Farewell" and his initials prominently displayed. After a sumptuous meal, club president Robert "Tug" Wilson offered the first in a long series of toasts to their departing comrade. They finished the evening by singing "Auld Lang Syne."[181]

The village of Mackinac Island offered diverse social opportunities to lure soldiers and their families out of the fort. As Mackinac Island became an increasingly popular summer resort in the 1880s, these social opportunities expanded. Fort residents flocked to the many traveling theatrical productions that visited the island. On May 30, 1887 soldiers and local citizens crowded into Fenton's Hall for the Royce-Lansing Musical Comedy Company presentation of *Private Tutors*. Two months later the crowd returned to the same venue for a performance by the Boston Comic Opera Company. Other forms of entertainment available in the village included concerts, dances and magic lantern shows.[182]

Social life often took enlisted men and officers in different directions. The caste system that existed between officers and their men was clearly evident in this social realm. While enlisted personnel socialized at the roller skating rink, crowded around the bar in Overall's Saloon or danced at one of the Astor House hops, officers and their wives waltzed at the Grand Hotel and attended receptions and dinner parties with civic leaders and island cottagers. With their dress blue uniforms and polished silver swords, fort officers were always included at the most elegant and festive affairs where they provided an air of military grandeur.

Along with sporting, recreational and social activities, fort soldiers also devoted free time to veterans organizations and island churches. The Civil War was the seminal military event for many soldiers of this period and a number of Fort Mackinac soldiers joined veterans groups. The Grand Army of the Republic (G.A.R.), founded in 1866, was an organization of Civil War veterans who shared wartime experiences while pursuing a political agenda that supported veterans benefits and patriotic causes. The Mackinac Island G.A.R. post was established in the mid-1880s and named in honor of Henry C. Pratt, the last commander of Fort Mackinac before the war and father of Twenty-third Infantry Lieutenant Edward B. Pratt. William Preston, saloon owner and former Fort Mackinac soldier, served as the post's first commander. His comrades were other retired veterans who lived on the island as well as active enlisted men who joined the post while serving at the fort. Island G.A.R. members proudly participated in the annual Decoration Day ceremonies on the island and in St. Ignace. Although considerably smaller than the G.A.R., the Military Order of the Loyal Legion of the United States was a veterans organization for former Union officers. Founded in 1865, the group counted about 8,000 members in the late 1890s. Many Fort Mackinac officers belonged to the Loyal Legion during this period but they participated in few activities except for Dr. John Bailey and Captain George Brady who attended a legion meeting in Grand Rapids in September 1885.[183]

Many soldiers joined Mackinac Island churches and several officers became active parish leaders. Between 1842 and 1861 the army provided for the spiritual needs of Fort Mackinac soldiers by assigning a full time chaplain to the post. During this period Rev. John O'Brien ministered to the needs of the garrison and offered weekly services in the post chapel on the second floor of the soldiers barracks. An ordained Episcopal minister, O'Brien's services were open to the local community. When soldiers returned to the island after the Civil War they initially worshiped in the village churches. In June 1869 Captain Leslie Smith, noting that there were "two houses of worship (a Roman Catholic and Methodist) in the town of Mackinac," ordered the church call beaten every Sunday morning at 10:30. Smith "earnestly recommended" that both officers and enlisted men attend "Divine Service, at least once each Sabbath."[184]

Fort Mackinac officers and their wives (including Mrs. Leslie Smith, below) were instrumental in developing and supporting Trinity Episcopal Church shown here ca. 1886.

Three years later Captain Smith joined with local residents to reestablish an Episcopal congregation on the island, and refitted the fort chapel for their use. Smith was elected Senior Warden and his wife and former post surgeon Dr. Samuel Jessop became members of the choir. The congregation met in the post chapel until the room was needed for the second company of soldiers assigned to the fort after the creation of Mackinac National Park in 1875. Parishioners used the village court house while they raised money and searched for a site to construct their church. Lieutenant William Daugherty was elected chairman of the building committee, which may explain why Trinity Church was constructed at the base of Fort Hill in 1882.

Fort officers continued to support the Episcopal congregation after it moved to the village. Soldiers constructed some of the chancel furnishings and officers served on the vestry and helped with religious education. In the late 1880s Captain Greenleaf Goodale agreed to run the Sunday school and his wife Margaret taught the Bible class. Among the teachers drafted by Goodale were Edith and Alice Hamilton, daughters of East Bluff cottager Montgomery Hamilton. The Hamilton sisters went on to become very prominent in their fields. Edith was an educator and distinguished author of books on mythology including *The Greek Way* (1930) and *The Roman Way* (1932). Alice graduated from the University of Michigan Medical school in 1893, became an expert in occupational diseases and was chosen as Harvard University's first woman faculty member in 1919.[185]

Other soldiers attended Ste. Anne's Roman Catholic Church, which traced its roots to early Jesuit missionaries who brought Christianity to the Straits of Mackinac in the late seventeenth century. The church's baptismal, marriage and burial records bear testimony to the presence of many soldiers and their families in the life of the church during this period. The wedding of Lieutenant Thomas Sharpe and Helen Rice, niece of island merchant James Rice, was one of the premier social events of the summer of 1874. After the service at Ste. Anne's Church, the wedding party proceeded to the Rice residence where "music and dancing prevailed and all went 'Merry as a marriage bell' from the tying of the knot to the good-bye at Midnight." Sadly, Helen's name reappeared in the church register just ten years later when she was buried in the island's Catholic cemetery at thirty-two years of age.[186]

Conclusion

THE MORE THAN ONE-THOUSAND SOLDIERS who served at Fort Mackinac between 1867 and 1895 had a wide variety of experiences during their years on Mackinac Island. Some saw Mackinac as a dull and depressing post and could not wait to leave. For many more the fort and flourishing tourist village was the highlight of their military career. Some soldiers enjoyed frequent promotions and the approbation of their officers, others were constantly in trouble and spent more time in the prison cell than on the parade ground. Mackinac was a place of love, romance and marriage for dozens of lucky soldiers while others suffered through loneliness, separation or the heartbreak of love gone bad. A few spent their entire military career at Mackinac but, for most, service on the island was just a small part of a longer military career.

Soldiers took many paths after leaving Fort Mackinac. Some remained in the army and traveled with their regiment around the country and eventually to Cuba or the Philippine Islands. Many soldiers who enjoyed the peaceful ambiance of sentry duty at Fort Mackinac came to know the horrors of battle during the Spanish American War. Most officers rose in the commissioned ranks and a handful even became general officers who served through World War I. Most soldiers eventually returned to civilian life and several who married local girls became permanent Mackinac Island citizens. A few who left the army soon realized that a soldiers' barracks was the only place that would ever be "home" for them. Most soldiers made smooth transitions to civilian life including Robert "Tug" Wilson whose interesting career at Fort Mackinac included scheduling games for the fort baseball team and writing articles for the Cheboygan newspaper. The plucky Wilson moved to Chicago after leaving the service and founded a private mortgage and loan company. When he returned to visit the island in 1891 his friends discovered that the one-time Fort

Mackinac private was now a "man of means" whose personal check was good for more than ten-thousand dollars.[187]

The children of Fort Mackinac officers often found themselves returning to the army later in their lives. Greenleaf Goodale's son George served two tours of duty in the Philippines before he was assigned as Professor of Military Science at Mississippi A & M College. Calvin D. Cowles saw three of his sons join the army: William and David followed their father to the Military Academy at West Point and Calvin Jr. became a military surgeon. Likewise, Harold Corbusier entered the Medical Corps and, like his father, served as an army doctor for several years before going into private practice. His brother Philip started at the bottom, working his way up from private to sergeant before he was commissioned as a second lieutenant in 1900.

Daughters, too, who grew up among the men, music and muskets of Fort Mackinac returned to the army, usually as wives of soldiers. Edward and Kate Pratt's only child, Mary, was wedded to Lieutenant Townsend Whalen at Fort Crook, Nebraska in 1905. Mary carried many fond memories of Fort Mackinac where she lived for six years after arriving at the island post as a two-year old child in 1884. She delighted in recalling her life in the officers' stone quarters where four generations of her family had lived.

Mackinac always held a special place in Mary's heart. She longed to return to her childhood home but the opportunity did not come until the summer of 1934, fifty years after she first arrived. With her husband, daughter and son-in-law she walked through the village where many of her young friends had lived, strolled past Trinity Church where she attended Sunday School, trudged up Fort Hill the site of so many delightful sledding parties and finally arrived on the veranda of the officers' stone quarters. From here, Mary gazed over the shimmering blue waters of the Straits of Mackinac and remarked that it was as beautiful

William Cowles as a West Point cadet in 1902 (ABOVE) and Mary Louise Pratt.

as she remembered. Surrounded by the wonder and fascination of Mackinac, Mary was reminded why her mother often said that her happiest times in the army were spent at Fort Mackinac.

Appendix

Military Units and Commissioned Officers
at Fort Mackinac 1867-1895

Company B, Forty-third Regiment of Infantry, *25 Aug. 1867 – 12 May 1869*
    John Mitchell, Captain
    Edwin C. Gaskill, First Lieutenant
    Julius Stommell, 2nd Lieutenant

Company F, First Regiment of Infantry, *12 May 1869 – 21 June 1874*
    Leslie Smith, Captain
    John Leonard, First Lieutenant
    Thomas Sharpe, First Lieutenant
    Matthew Markland, 2nd Lieutenant

Company E, Twenty-second Regiment of Infantry,
    10 July 1874 – 14 July 1876 & 31 October 1877 – 14 May 1879
    Alfred L. Hough, Major
    Charles Dickey, Captain
    William Daugherty, 1st Lieutenant
    John McAdam Webster, 2nd Lieutenant

Company C, Twenty-second Regiment of Infantry,
    19 May 1876 – 24 July 1877
    Joseph Bush, Captain
    Thomas H. Fisher, 1st Lieutenant
    Fielding L. Davis, 2nd Lieutenant
    Theodore Mosher, Jr., 2nd Lieutenant

Company D, Twenty-second Regiment of Infantry,
    16 Oct 1877 – 14 May 1879
    Charles A. Webb, Captain
    Oscar D. Ladley, 1st Lieutenant
    John B. Ballance, 2nd Lieutenant

Major Charles Dickey

Company D, Tenth Regiment of Infantry, *24 May 1879 – 1 June 1884*
    Edwin E. Sellers, Captain
    Walter T. Duggan, 1st Lieutenant
    Bogardus Eldridge, 2nd Lieutenant
    John Adams Perry, 2nd Lieutenant

Company C, Tenth Regiment of Infantry, *31 May 1879 – 8 June 1884*
 Charles L. Davis, Captain
 Dwight Kelton, 1st Lieutenant
 Edward H. Plummer, 2nd Lieutenant

Company E, Twenty-third Regiment of Infantry, *6 June 1884 – 8 May 1890*
 George K. Brady, Captain
 William C. Manning, Captain
 Calvin D. Cowles, 1st Lieutenant
 Edward B. Pratt, 1st Lieutenant, *1889-90*
 Benjamin Clark Morse, 2nd Lieutenant

Company K, Twenty-third Regiment of Infantry, *11 June 1884 – 8 May 1890*
 Greenleaf A. Goodale, Captain
 Edward B. Pratt, Lieutenant, *1884-89*
 Stephen O'Conner, 2nd Lieutenant
 George B. Davis, 2nd Lieutenant

Company C, Nineteenth Regiment of Infantry, *6 May 1890 – 9 Oct 1894*
  & 16 Sept 1895
 Charles T. Witherell, Captain
 Woodbridge Geary, 1st Lieutenant
 Joseph Frazier, 2nd Lieutenant
 Zebulon Vance, 2nd Lieutenant

Company D, Nineteenth Regiment of Infantry, *5 May 1890 – 27 Nov 1892*
 Jacob H. Smith, Captain
 Alexander M. Guard, Captain
 Edmund D. Smith, 1st Lieutenant
 Henry G. Learned, 2nd Lieutenant
 Edwin M. Coates, Major
 Clarence E. Bennett, Major

Medical Officers:

Dr. Hiram Mills, Acting Assistant Surgeon*	*1868-1870*
Dr. Samuel Jessop, Captain, Assistant Surgeon	*1870*
Dr. John R. Bailey, Acting Assistant Surgeon*	*1871*
Dr. William M. Notson, Captain, Assistant Surgeon	*1872-1873*
Dr. Carlos Carvallo, Captain, Assistant Surgeon	*1873*
Dr. John R. Bailey, Acting Assistant Surgeon*	*1873*
Dr. Jenne Victor De Hanne, Captain, Assistant Surgeon	*1874-1876*
Dr. John R. Bailey, Acting Assistant Surgeon*	*1876*
Dr. Peter Moffat, Captain, Assistant Surgeon	*1877-1879*
Dr. John R. Bailey, Acting Assistant Surgeon*	*1879*
Dr. G.W. Adair, Captain, Assistant Surgeon	*1879-1881*
Dr. John R. Bailey, Acting Assistant Surgeon*	*1881*
Dr. William H. Corbusier, Captain, Assistant Surgeon	*1882-1884*
Dr. John R. Bailey, Acting Assistant Surgeon*	*1884*
Dr. Charles E. Woodruff, 1st Lieutenant, Acting Surgeon	*1887-1889*
Dr. John R. Bailey, Acting Assistant Surgeon*	*1889*
Dr. Harlan McVay, Acting Assistant Surgeon*	*1889*
Dr. Harlan McVay, 1st Lieutenant, Assistant Surgeon	*1889-91*
Dr. John R. Bailey, Acting Assistant Surgeon*	*1891*
Dr. Edwin F. Gardner, Captain, Assistant Surgeon	*1892*
Dr. John R. Bailey, Attending Surgeon*	*1894-1895*

* Dr. Hiram Mills, Dr. Harlan McVay and Dr. John R. Bailey were private physicians. "Acting Assistant Surgeon" is the title given a civilian physician serving as a contractual post surgeon. Dr. Bailey had prior (1854) service at Fort Mackinac as an army post surgeon.

Fort Mackinac ca. 1890

Acknowledgements

This book would not have been possible without the considerable contributions of many individuals. Kyle Bagnall, Violet Bowling, Katie Cederholm, Robert J. Fletcher, Roy Goodale, Dennis Havlena, Bruce Hawkins, Andrew Jones, Bruce Lynn, Rick Robyn, Craig Scott and Keith Widder provided research assistance. David Armour, Steve Brisson, Lynn Evans, Carl Nold and Tim Putman reviewed the manuscript and made valuable suggestions and contributions to the final product. I am deeply grateful for all of the help and encouragement that they provided.

Notes

1 Calvin D. Cowles to C.J. Cowles, 18 July 1884. C.J. Cowles Papers, Southern Historical Collection, University of North Carolina at Chapel Hill.

2 Information about the fort during this period is found in "Inspection Reports (1869, 1870, 1871), Records of the Officer of the Inspector General," RG 159, Selected Inspection Reports, Fort Mackinac, 1824-1890. National Archives, (hereinafter cited as ROIG); "Medical History, Fort Mackinac, Michigan 1871 – 1877," 13-30. Records of the Adjutant General's Office, RG 94, National Archives, (hereinafter cited as MHFM).

3 James B. Fry to Assistant Adjutant General, 8 September 1875, "Consolidated Correspondence File on Fort Mackinac, Michigan, 1819-1890," Records of the Office of the Quartermaster General, RG 92, National Archives, (hereinafter cited as ROQG).

4 Correspondence of the Fort Mackinac Quartermaster, 1874-1877, ROQG; "Historic Structures Report, Sergeants' Quarters, Fort Mackinac." Mackinac Island State Park Commission, September 1994, 5-7, 9-10.

5 "Historic Structures Report, Soldiers' Barracks, Fort Mackinac," 11-12.

6 Jack D. Foner, *The United States Soldier Between Two Wars: Army Life and Reforms, 1865-1898* (New York: Humanities Press, 1970) 77-79.

7 Foner, 78-79, 92-94; William Manning to Adjutant General, 31 December 1889, Vol. 18, FMLS.

8 Journal entry, Dr. John R. Bailey, 13 May 1885, MHFM.

9 D. H. Kelton to Chief Quartermaster, 31 December 1883, ROQG.

10 Journal entries, Dr. John R. Bailey, 30 November 1885 and 31 December 1885, MHFM.

11 Order No. 118, October 8, 1889. "Records of United States Army Commands (Army Posts), Fort Mackinac Michigan," RG 393, National Archives. (Hereinafter cited as USAC)

12 Order No. 46, June 7, 1886 and Order No. 48, 11 June 1886, USAC. Telegram from G. A. Goodale to City Marshall, Cheboygan, 6 June 1886, "Letters Sent," Vol. 16. "Records of the United States Army Continental Commands," RG 393, National Archives, (hereinafter cited as FMLS)

13 *Cheboygan Democrat*, 29 July 1886.

14 "Order No. 2," 21 January 1878, USAC.

15 Phyllis Corbusier Pierson, ed. "Recollections of Her Life in the Army," unpublished manuscript by Fanny Dunbar Corbusier, 1959: 82, U.S. Army Military History Institute, Carlisle Barracks, Penn.

16 Foner, 2.

17 One thousand and eight soldiers served at Fort Mackinac during this period including 928 enlisted men, 54 officers (10 were medical officers) and 26 general staff and hospital corps non-commissioned officers.

18 The following regiments served at Fort Mackinac during this period: Forty-third Infantry 1867-1869, First Infantry 1869-1874, Twenty-second Infantry 1874-1879, Tenth Infantry 1879-1884, Twenty-third Infantry 1884-1890 and Nineteenth Infantry 1890-1895.

19 Colonel Richard I. Dodge, "The Enlisted Soldier," *Journal of Military Service Institution*,

VIII, (September 1887): 263.

20   "Fort Mackinac Muster Rolls," Companies C and D Tenth Infantry, August 1893, Fort Mackinac Muster Rolls, Records of the Adjutant General's Office, RG 94, National Archives (Hereinafter cited as FMMR).

21   Edward M. Coffman, *The Old Army, A Portrait of the American Army in Peacetime, 1784-1898*, (New York: Oxford University Press, 1986,) 336-340. 45; Don Rickey, *Forty Miles at Day on Beans and Hay, The Enlisted Soldier Fighting the Indian Wars*, (Norman: University of Oklahoma Press, 1963,) 33-49.

22   Dodge, 264.

23   "Fort Mackinac Muster Rolls," Companies C and D, Nineteenth, Infantry, March-April, 1892, FMMR.

24   "Fort Mackinac Muster Rolls," Companies C and D, Tenth Infantry, 1893, FMMR; "Register of Enlistments," 1878-1884, reels 41-43, USROE; Walter Duggan to John Orin, 12 March 1883, FMLS.

25   "Fort Mackinac Muster Rolls," Companies E and K, Twenty-third Infantry, 1885-1889, FMMR.

26   "Fort Mackinac Muster Rolls," Companies C and D, Nineteenth Infantry, 1890-1894, FMMR.

27   Coffman, 330.

28   "Register of Enlistments," 1867-1897, reels 33-48, USROE.

29   *Ibid.*

30   "Summary Court Record, Hugh Stevenson," 17 August 1892, FMSCR; "Fort Mackinac, General Court Martial of Henry Pedigrew," 10 February 1888, Fort Mackinac. "Records of the Judge Advocate General," RG 153, National Archives, (hereinafter cited as RJAG); "General Court Martial of Martin Curley," 10 January 1888, Fort Mackinac, RJAG; "Garrison Court Martial of Martin Boyle," Order No. 44, 12 May 1888, USAC.

31   The ages of Fort Mackinac's enlisted men is taken from the Register of Enlistments, Reels 33-48, USROE.

32   "Theodore Reiths, Register of Enlistments," 1871-1877, reel 40, USROE; "General Court Martial of John Monroe," 18 April 1878, RJAG; "Fort Mackinac Muster Roll," Company E Twenty-second Infantry, February 1879, FMMR.

33   "Patrick McCormick, Register of Enlistments," 1893-1897, reel 48, USROE.

34   Coffman, 397. Foner, 72.

35   Leslie Smith to Adjutant General, U.S. Army, 6 February 1871, "Letters Sent, Vol. 11," FMLS.

36   "Register of Enlistments," Reels 33-48, USROE.

37   "Return of Company C," Twenty-second Infantry, January 1877; "Fort Mackinac Post Returns," 1816-1895; "Records of the War Department, Office of the Adjutant General," National Archives, (hereinafter cited as FMPR)

38   "Register of Enlistments, 1867-1897," reels 33-48, "United States Register of Enlistments," microfilm copy number 233, National Archives, (hereinafter cited as USROE).

39   "Register of Enlistments, 1867-1897," reels 33-48, USROE.

40   "Fort Mackinac Muster Roll," Company D, Twenty-second Infantry, September-October 1878, FMMR.

41   "Pension file, Thomas H. Ferris," United States Army Pension Files, National Archives, Washington, D.C.

42   "Order No. 14," 16 March 1887, USAC.

43   "Mackinac County Census, 1880," National Archives; "Fort Mackinac Muster Rolls," Company D, Tenth Infantry, August-September, 1881, FMMR.

44 Rickey, 126-127.

45 Coffman, 346.

46 Coffman, 346; Foner, 16.

47 Leslie Smith to Assistant Adjutant General, Headquarters, Department of the Lakes, 1 July 1872, FMLS.

48 Coffman 347; Foner 16-17; Rickey 95, 110.

49 "Fort Mackinac Muster Rolls," Companies E and K, Twenty-third Infantry, 1884-1890, FMMR; "Register of Enlistments," 1878-1890, reels 41-45, USROE.

50 "Fort Mackinac Muster Rolls," Company E, Twenty-third Infantry, September-October 1887 – July-August 1889; Company C, Nineteenth Infantry, July-August 1891, September-October 1894, FMMR.

51 "Summary Court Record, William Bennett," 13 July 1891, "Summary Court Records, 1890-1894." Records of the Adjutant General's Office, RG 94, National Archives, (hereinafter cited as FMSCR).

52 Dr. John R. Bailey, "Medical History Fort Mackinac," January 1886, MHFM.

53 "Order No. 13," 24 January 1889, USAC.

54 "Summary Court Martial, Edward Bruckner," 18 March 1891, FMSCR.

55 "Fort Mackinac Muster Rolls," Company D, Nineteenth Infantry, March-April, 1891; *The Soldiers Handbook: For the Use of the Enlisted Men of the Army*, (Washington, D.C.: Government Printing Office, 1884.) Original copy belonging to James B. Martin in collection of Mackinac State Historic Parks.

56 Character evaluations are found in the "Register of Enlistments, 1867-1897," reels 33-48, USROE and "Fort Mackinac Muster Rolls, 1877-1895," FMMR.

57 "Fort Mackinac Muster Rolls," Company D, Nineteenth Infantry, March-April 1891, FMMR.

58 Joseph Frazier to John B. Fletcher, 27 February 1893, John B. Fletcher collection, Mackinac State Historic Parks.

59 Major Roy Goodale, "A Family Affair, Four Generations in Uniform." *Military Images*, Vol. , No. 5, (March-April, 1990): 21-23.

60 Roy Goodale, Interview by author, Mackinac Island, Mich. 7 July 1988, Mackinac State Historic Parks Archives.

61 Phil Porter, "Mackinac Island's Post Cemetery," (Mackinac Island: Mackinac State Historic Parks, 1999,) 4-5.

62 Francis B. Heitman, *Historical Register and Dictionary of the United States Army, 1789-1903*, Volume 1, (Washington: Government Printing House, 1903); Norman Stevens, "Commissioned Officers of the Army of the United States at Fort Mackinac," unpublished manuscript, Mackinac State Historic Parks.

63 Ibid.

64 Ibid.

65 Heitman, 688.

66 Heitman, 753.

67 Stevens, "William H. Corbusier" and "Edwin F. Gardner."

68 Bailey, John R. M.D. *Mackinac, Formerly Michilimackinac, History and Guidebook*, (Grand Rapids: Tradesman Company, 1909,) 9-11; William Manning to Assistant Adjutant General, 20 April 1889, FMLS.

69 Stevens, "Harlan E. McVay."

70 "General Orders No. 5 and 7;" "Special Orders No. 17 and 19," 1869, USAC.

71 Matthew Markland to William Notson, 16 August 1873, FMLS.

72   Journal entry, Dr. Carlos Carvallo, October, 1873, MHFM.

73   Leslie Smith, "Circular to Saloon Keepers, Mackinac, Mich.," 19 March 1870, FMLS.

74   Leslie Smith to John R. Bailey, Trustee of Union School, Mackinac, Michigan, 22 April 1870, FMLS.

75   Leslie Smith to Acting Assist Adjutant General, Department of the Lakes, 10 June 1869, FMLS.

76   "Inspection Reports," 1869-1890, ROIG.

77   "Inspection Report," 1887, ROIG.

78   W. J. Duggan to D.H. Kelton, 20 December 1882, FMLS.

79   "Fort Mackinac Muster Rolls," Company B, Forty-third Infantry, March-November 1868; Company C, Tenth Infantry, September 1881-October 1883; Company E, Twenty-third Infantry, June 1884-July 1887; Company D, Infantry, June 1881-May 1883; Company K, Twenty-third Infantry May-June 1888 and November-December 1888; Company K, Twenty-third Infantry, August 1889-May 1890, FMMR; "Special Order No. 36," 29 August 1875, USAC.

80   Calvin D. Cowles to C.J. Cowles, 26 May 1880, C.J. Cowles Papers, Southern Historical Collection, University of North Carolina at Chapel Hill.

81   *Ibid*, Calvin D. Cowles to C.J. Cowles, 24 June 1883 and 14 July 1887.

82   Coffman, 281.

83   "Efficiency Report of Charles T. Witherell," 1 March 1894; "Efficiency Report of Thomas Sharpe," 1 May 1890 and 30 June 1895, copies in Mackinac State Historic Parks library.

84   Journal entry, Dr. John R. Bailey, July 1885, MHFM.

85   "Orders, No. 76, 6 November 1879, USAC

86   Journal entries, Dr. J.V. DeHanne, January 1875, April 1875, October 1875 and April 1877, MHFM.

87   Journal entry, Dr. Charles Woodruff, June 1893, MHFM.

88   Journal entry, Dr. J.V. DeHanne, November 1874, MHFM.

89   "Consolidated Report of the Sick and Wounded of the Army Serving at Fort Mackinac, 1885-1894," Records of the Adjutant General's Office, RG 94, National Archives.

90   Journal entry, Dr. Charles E. Woodruff, 31 August 1887, MHFM.

91   Journal entries, Dr. Harlan McVay, January 1890 and April 1891, MHFM.

92   Journal entries, Dr. John Bailey, March 1885 and January 1886, MHFM.

93   Journal entry, Dr. John Bailey, May 1887, MHFM.

94   Journal entry, Dr. Charles Woodruff, September 1887, MHFM.

95   Journal entry, Dr. George Adair, March 1881, MHFM; "Orders, No. 14," 16 March 1881, USAC.

96   Journal entry, Dr. Carlos Carvallo, July 1874, MHFM.

97   "Orders No. 24," 9 April 1884, USAC; Pierson, 86.

98   Journal entry, Dr. John R. Bailey, June 1887, MHFM.

99   "Description of the Post," Dr. Carlos Carvallo, 30 April 1784, MHFM.

100 Journal entry, Dr. John Bailey, April 1882, MHFM.

101 Journal entries, Dr. Carlos Carvallo, Vol. 150: 68 (n.d.); Dr. John Bailey, March & July, 1885; Dr. Harlan McVay, 12 October 1891, MHFM.

102 "Fort Mackinac Inspection Report," 4 August 1888, ROIG.

103 "Orders No. 51," 7 July 1887, USAC.

104 "Orders No. 5," 18 February 1887, USAC.

105 "Orders, No. 76," 6 November 1879, USAC.

106 "Orders, No. 2," 13 January 1879, USAC.

107 Edwin E. Sellers to Assistant Adjutant General, Department of the East, 19 August 1883; George Brady to Assistant Adjutant General, Department of the East, 12 August 1885, FMLS.

108 "Orders No. 28," 24 February 1889, USAC; "Inspection Report, 1889," ROIG.

109 Coffman, 276; "Post Lyceum," 3 November 1891 – 26 April 1894. Records of the Adjutant General's Office, RG 94, National Archives.

110 "Guard Roster of troops stationed at Fort Mackinac, Michigan," 18 May 1883, Records of the Adjutant General's Office, RG 94, National Archives.

111 "General Court Martial of John Lambert," 26 July 1879, RJAG.

112 "Order No. 20," 19 March 1886, USAC.

113 "General Court Martial of Frank Darlington," 23 November 1888 and "General Court Martial of Henry Pedigrew," 24 November 1888, RJAG.

114 Journal entry, Dr. John R. Bailey, 31 January 1887, MHFM.

115 Jacob Smith to Adjutant General U.S.A., Washington D.C., 27 August 1890, FMLS.

116 John S. Billings, *Circular No. 8, Report on the Hygiene of the United States Army*, (Washington, D. C. War Department, Surgeon-General's Office, 1875,) xlv.

117 Journal entry, Dr. Charles Woodruff, June, 1893, MHFM; "Inspection Reports," 1886, 1887, 1888, ROIG; Keith Widder, *Reveille Till Taps, Soldier Life at Fort Mackinac, 1780-1895*, (Mackinac Island, Michigan: Mackinac Island State Park Commission, 1972) 62-63.

118 Journal entries, Dr. Charles Woodruff, January-December 1892, MHFM.

119 Journal entries, Dr. J.V. DeHanne, October 1875, Dr. Charles Woodruff, June 1893, MHFM.

120 Pierson, 84.

121 Grace F. Kane, "Recollections of Early Days at Mackinac," *Michigan History Magazine*, Vol. X (1926): 334-335.

122 "Individual Ledger, G.T. Arnold," 1888-1889, Mackinac State Historic Parks.

123 "Order No. 7," 23 June 1871, USAC.

124 "Order No. 32," 21 June 1881, USAC.

125 "Order No. 53," 30 December 1877, USAC; Greenleaf Goodale to Assistant Adjutant General, Division of the Atlantic, 11 September 1889, FMLS.

126 "Order No. 15," 22 September 1869, USAC.

127 Douglas McChristian, *An Army of Marksmen*, (Fort Collins: The Old Army Press, 1981) 21-60.

128 George Brady to Assistant Adjutant General, Department of the East, 1 August 1885, FMLS; "Inspection Reports," 1887-1888, ROIG.

129 "Order No. 51," 31 August 1885, USAC; "Register of Marksmanship of Military Personnel in Small Arms, 1887-1889," Records of the Headquarters of the Army, Entry 56, RG 108, National Archives.

130 Journal entries, Dr. John R. Bailey, July & August 1885, MHFM.

131 "Fort Mackinac Muster Rolls," Company E, Twenty-second Infantry, July–August 1876, FMMR.

132 Stevens, "Harlan E. McVay," "Theodore Mosher," "Woodbridge Geary," "Charles Woodruff."

133 Journal entries, Dr. J.V. DeHanne, July 1876 and Dr. Edwin Gardner, June 1893, MHFM.

134 "Orders No. 29," 11 May 1887; No. 35, 29 April 1888 and No. 90, 24 August 1888, USAC.

135 "Record of Passes Granted," 9 November 1882, 9 August 1883, Fort Mackinac, Records of the Adjutant General's Office, RG 94, National Archives.

136 "Order No. 9," 22 April 1875 and Order No. 47, 18 June 1884, USAC; "General Court Martial of Charles Smith," 14 May 1889, RJAG.

137 Foner, 91; "Circular," 29 November 1879 and "Order No. 72," 20 June 1889, USAC.

138 "Order No. 14," 3 July 1873, USAC.

139 *Cheboygan Democrat*, 8 July 1886.

140 "General Courts Martial of Joseph Johnson and Fredrick Lane," 24 July 1872, RJAG.

141 "General Court Martial of Captain Joseph Bush," 8 August 1876, RJAG.

142 Journal entry, Dr. Charles Woodruff, September 1887, MHFM.

143 "General Court Martial of John Lyons," 22 November 1883, RJAG.

144 "Orders No. 2," 3 January 1889; No. 17, 29 January 1889 and No. 20, 8 February 1889, USAC; "General Court Martial of Henry L. Coon," 14 May 1889, RJAG.

145 Greenleaf Goodale to Assistant Adjutant General, Division of the Atlantic, 31 August 1887, FMLS.

146 Alfred Hough to Willis Swift, 27 January 1878, FMLS.

147 "General Court Martial of William Bowman," 16 July 1873, RJAG.

148 Coffman, 371.

149 "Fort Mackinac Muster Rolls," Company E, Twenty-second Infantry, January-June 1878, FMMR.

150 "General Courts Martial of George Cain," 14 July 1873 and Thomas Mullin, 12 July 1873, RJAG.

151 George Brady to Assistant Adjutant General, Department of the East, 12 August 1884, FMLS.

152 Greenleaf Goodale to Assistant Adjutant General, Division of the Atlantic, 18 August 1886, FMLS.

153 Dodge, 262.

154 Foner, 111; Coffman, 374.

155 "Fort Mackinac Muster Roll," Company C, Nineteenth Infantry, May-June 1891 & March-April, 1893, FMMR.

156 Coffman, 374.

157 "Orders No. 5," 4 April 1873 & No. 47, 19 May 1891, USAC; "Summary Court Martial, William Sullivan," 7 August 1893, FMSCR.

158 "Liber 1, Marriage Records of Mackinac County, 1867-1887," Mackinac County Courthouse, St. Ignace, Mich.; Mackinac County, Mich. U.S. Censuses, Mackinac County, Michigan, 1870 and 1880.

159 Stevens, "Charles A. Webb" and "John McAdam Webster;" *Flint Journal*, 1 October 1942.

160 U.S. Censuses, Mackinac County, Michigan, 1870 and 1880.

161 Edwin Coates to Adjutant, Nineteenth Infantry, Fort Wayne, Michigan, 11 June 1891, FMLS.

162 "General Court Martial of Captain Joseph Bush," 4 August 1876, RJAG.

163 "Inspection Report, 1872," ROIG; "Order No. 1," 11 February 1870, USAC.

164 Thomas Wilhelm, *A Military Dictionary and Gazetteer,* (Philadelphia: L.R. Hammersly and Co., 1881) 312; "Order No. 8," 30 December 1879, USAC.

165 C.D. Cowles to C.J. Cowles, 30 May 1878; 23 June 1878; 18 July 1884; 18 November 1887, C.J. Cowles Papers, Southern Historical Collection, University of North Carolina

at Chapel Hill.

166 Mary E. Cowles to Mrs. C.J. Cowles, 26 April 1883, C.J. Cowles Papers, Southern Historical Collection, University of North Carolina at Chapel Hill.

167 C.D. Cowles to C.J. Cowles, 5 September 1884, C.J. Cowles Papers, Southern Historical Collection, University of North Carolina at Chapel Hill.

168 Phil Porter, Ed., *A Boy at Fort Mackinac, The Diary of Harold Dunbar Corbusier, 1883-1884, 1892,* (Mackinac Island: The Corbusier Archives and Mackinac Island State Park Commission, 1994.)

169 "Order No. 63," 24 September 1879, USAC.

170 John Mitchell to H. Clay Wood, Assistant Adjutant General, Department of the Lakes, 24 February 1868; E. E. Sellers to Assistant Adjutant General, Department of the East, 19 August 1883, FMLS; Pierson, 83.

171 "Inspection Report," 1888, ROIG.

172 "Fund of the Fort Mackinac Base Ball Club," Roster 1885 and 1890-1893, Records of the Adjutant General's Office, RG 94, National Archives.

173 Journal Entry, Dr. John R. Bailey, July 1885, MHFM.

174 Journal Entry, Dr. John R. Bailey, August 1885, MHFM.

175 *Cheboygan Democrat,* 7 July 1887.

176 *Cheboygan Democrat,* 22 July 1886 and 26 August 1886.

177 "Circular," 13 August 1875, USAC.

178 Charles Foster to Mr. Nicholas Shomin, 31 October 1892, copy in collection of Mackinac State Historic Parks. E. M. Coates to Assistant Adjutant General, Department of the Missouri, 22 January 1892, FMLS.

179 Pierson, 84-5; Diary of Richard Hulbert, 4 February 1889, microfilm copy in collection of Mackinac State Historic Parks.

180 Pierson, 85; Grace F. Kane, 346.

181 *Cheboygan Democrat,* 22 December 1887; *St. Ignace News,* 24 February 1888.

182 *Cheboygan Democrat,* 26 May 1887 and 21 July 1887.

183 Journal Entry, Dr. John R. Bailey, September 1885, MHFM.

184 "Order No. 6," 5 June 1869, USAC.

185 Alice Hamilton to Agnes Hamilton, Mackinaw, 21 July 1889, Hamilton Family Letters, 1818-1970, 1974, (MC 278), roll 29: folders 624-642, Schlesinger Library, Radcliff College, Cambridge, Mass.

186 John Bates to Mr. Horatio Crain, 7 July 1874, "Letter Book," business correspondence of Mackinac Island Merchants, Alexander Toll (July 1852); Bromilow and Bates, 1869-1874. Original in collections of Mackinac State Historic Parks.

187 "Richard Hulbert Diary, 1887-1891," 1891, 155-56.

Index

McCormick, Patrick, 28, 29, 35
McGrath, John, 53
McGulpin, Annie, 80
McGulpin, Benjamin, 80
McManus, James 79
McNamara, Jane, 83
McNamara, Patrick, 35, 83
McVay, Dr. Harlan, 41, 51, 55, 69, 102
McVay, Flora, 55, 69
Meals, 49, 61-65, 70, 71
Merrill, James, 30
Mess hall, 49, 70
Military Order of the Loyal Legion, 95
Mills, Dr. Hiram, 40, 102
Minosky, Max, 30
Mirandette, Antoine, 80
Mission House, 42
Mitchell, John, 10, 15, 28, 39, 43, 65, 88, 100
Mitchell, Peter, 51
Moffat, Dr. Peter, 102
Monroe, Duncan, 35
Monroe, John, 28
Morse, Benjamin, 79, 82, 83, 101
Mosher, Theodore, 69, 100
Mullin, Thomas, 76

N

Nineteenth Infantry, 23, 26, 29, 35, 40, 56, 70
Non-commissioned officers, 18, 27, 28, 30-34, 37, 72, 84
Notson, Dr. William, 40, 42, 102

O

O'Brien, Rev. John, 95,
O'Conner, Stephen, 101
Officers Lyceum, 58
Owen, Abraham, 35

P

Packard, Charles, 37

Paquette, C. S., 77
Parade ground, 16-18, 48, 56, 58, 65, 66, 70, 71, 84, 90
Passes, 70
Pauly, Louis, 85
Pauly, Nettie, 85
Pay rates, 33-35, 45, 46
Pedigrew, Henry, 27, 45, 61
Perry, John Adams, 100
Perry, Mrs. Lewis, 84
Philippine Islands, 69, 99
Phillips, Henry, 79
Plummer, Edward, 65, 101
Plummer, Mrs., 93
Police duty, 21, 35, 71
Pratt, Edward, 26, 39, 47, 82, 89, 90, 95, 99, 101
Pratt, Henry, 95
Pratt, Kate, 94, 99
Pratt, Mary, 86, 99
Preston, William, 95

R

Raymond, Edward, 33, 75
Recruiting, 24-26, 45
Register of Enlistments, 26, 28, 29
Reiths, Theodore, 28
Reynolds, John, 28
Rice, James, 97
Rifle matches, 47, 71
Rifle range, 21, 43, 48, 66-68
Robinson, George, 21, 61, 75
Rogers, Anna, 54
Rogers, Judson, 54
Romanis, John, 31
Romans, William, 30
Ryan, Jerry, 88
Ryan, Joanna, 88
Ryan, William, 88

S

Schofield, General John M., 58